Network Practices

Anthony Burke and Therese Tierney, editors

Network Practices

New Strategies in Architecture and Design

Princeton Architectural Press, New York
www.papress.com

Published by
Princeton Architectural Press
37 East Seventh Street
New York, New York 10003

For a free catalog of books, call 1.800.722.6657.
Visit our web site at www.papress.com.

Editor: Scott Tennent
Content editor: Ron Nyren
Design: Jan Haux

Special thanks to: Nettie Aljian, Sara Bader, Dorothy Ball, Nicola
Bednarek, Janet Behning, Becca Casbon, Penny (Yuen Pik) Chu, Russell
Fernandez, Pete Fitzpatrick, Sara Hart, Clare Jacobson, John King,
Mark Lamster, Nancy Eklund Later, Linda Lee, Katharine Myers, Lauren
Nelson Packard, Jennifer Thompson, Joseph Weston, and Deb Wood of
Princeton Architectural Press —Kevin C. Lippert, publisher

Library of Congress Cataloging-in-Publication Data
Network practices : new strategies in architecture and design / Anthony
Burke and Therese Tierney, editors. — 1st ed.
p. cm.
Includes bibliographical references.
ISBN 1-56898-701-3 (alk. paper)
1. Architecture and technology. 2. Design and technology. 3. Computer
networks. I. Burke, Anthony, 1970- II. Tierney, Therese.
NA2543.T43N48 2007
720.285'465-dc22
2006036320

Table of Contents

Preface
25   Anthony Burke and Therese Tierney

The Architectural Brain
30   Mark Wigley

Redefining Network Paradigms
54   Anthony Burke

Biological Networks:
On Neurons, Cellular Automata,
and Relational Architectures
78   Therese Tierney

Scalar Networks, Super Creeps:
Approaching the Non-Standard
in the Architecture of Servo
100   Christopher Hight

Stop Motion Studies
116   David Crawford

Material Agency
120   Peter Testa and Devyn Weiser

The Dom-in(f)o House

132 Dagmar Richter

From Data to Its Organizing Structure

144 George Legrady

Beyond Code

166 C. E. B. Reas

Climbing through Complexity Ceilings

178 Peter J. Bentley

Multi-National City: Inside Outsourcing

198 Reinhold Martin

Intelligence After Theory

212 Michael Speaks

218 Acknowledgments

220 Image Credits

222 Contributor Biographies

A short visual introduction to Network Practices:

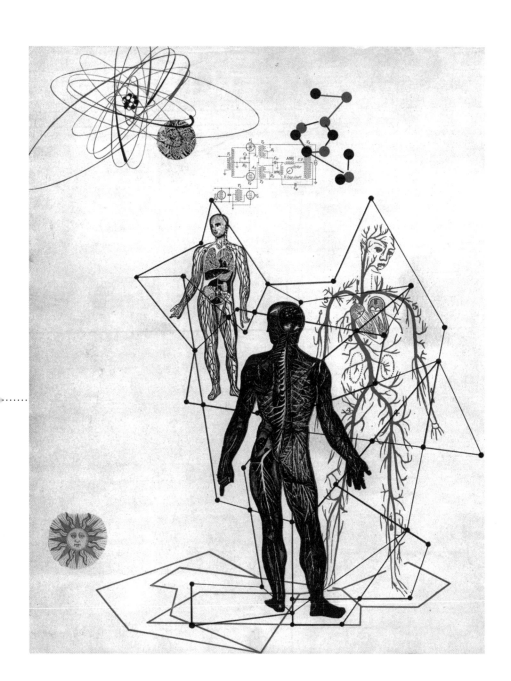

from:
The Architectural Brain
see p. 51

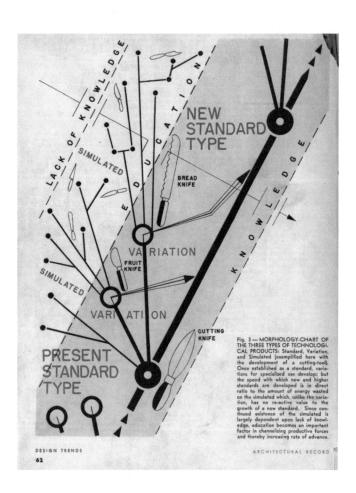

NEW STANDARD TYPE

BREAD KNIFE

VARIATION

FRUIT KNIFE

VARIATION

CUTTING KNIFE

PRESENT STANDARD TYPE

LACK OF KNOWLEDGE

SIMULATED

EDUCATION

KNOWLEDGE

SIMULATED

Fig. 3 — MORPHOLOGY-CHART OF THE THREE TYPES OF TECHNOLOGICAL PRODUCTS: Standard, Variation, and Simulated (exemplified here with the development of a cutting-tool). Once established as a standard, variations for specialized use develop: but the speed with which new and higher standards are developed is in direct ratio to the amount of energy wasted on the simulated which, unlike the variation, has no re-active value to the growth of a new standard. Since continued existence of the simulated is largely dependent upon lack of knowledge, education becomes an important factor in channelizing productive forces and thereby increasing rate of advance.

DESIGN TRENDS
62

ARCHITECTURAL RECORD

from:
The Architectural Brain
see p. 51

from:
Redefining Network Paradigms
see p. 69

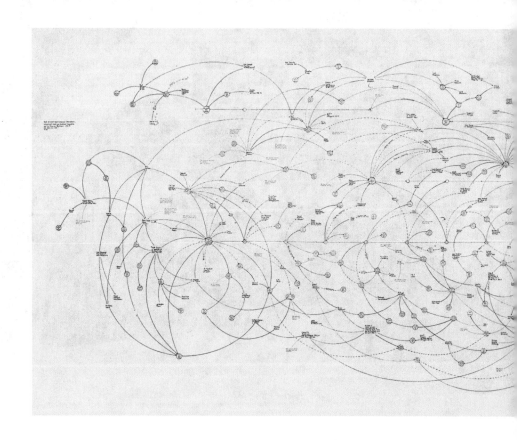

from:
Redefining Network Paradigms
see p. 64-65

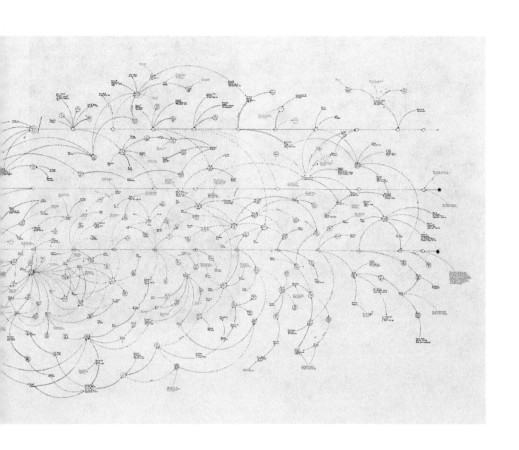

13

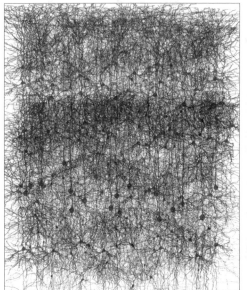 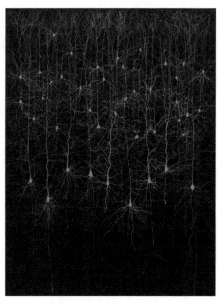

from:
Biological Networks: On Neurons, Cellular
Automata, and Relational Architectures
see p. 91

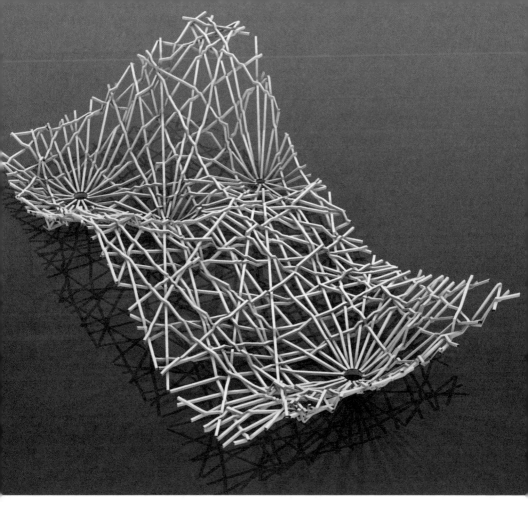

from:
Biological Networks: On Neurons, Cellular
Automata, and Relational Architectures
see p. 95

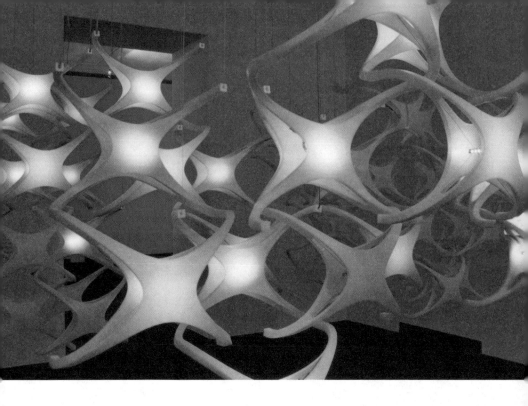

from:
Scalar Networks, Super Creeps:
Approaching the Non-Standard in the
Architecture of Servo
see p. 111

from:
Stop Motion Studies
see p. 117

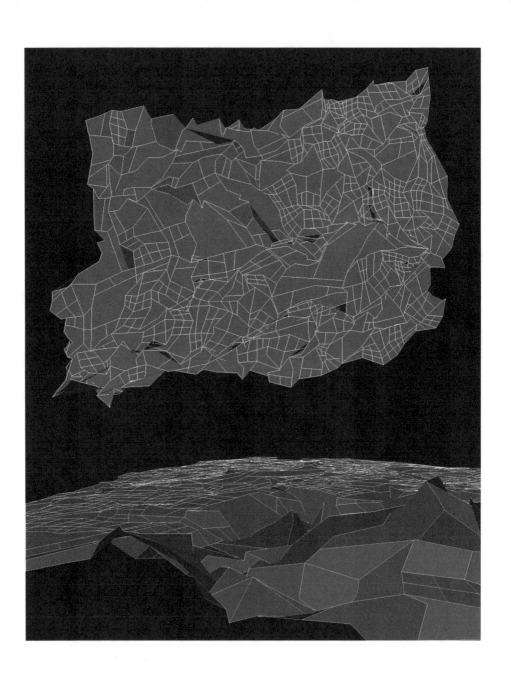

from:
Material Agency
see p. 127

from:
The Dom-in(f)o House
see p. 137

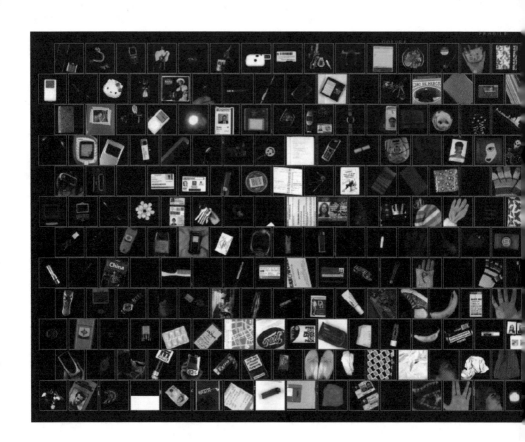

from:
From Data to Its Organizing Structure
see p. 156-157

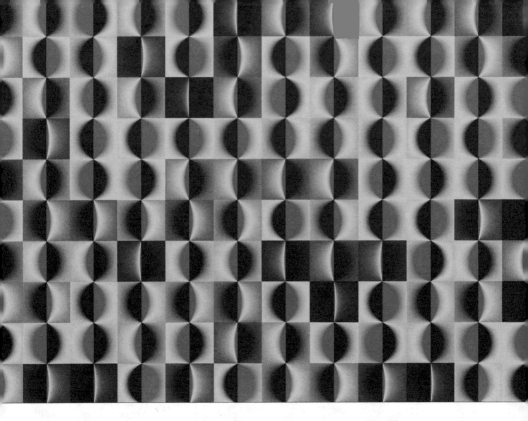

from:
From Data to Its Organizing Structure
see p. 163

from:
Beyond Code
see p. 173

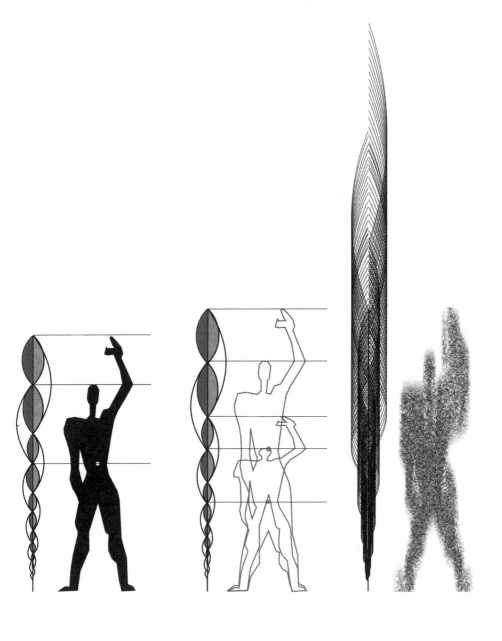

from:
Multi-National City
see p. 207

Introduction

Anthony Burke and Therese Tierney

Network structures have fast become the organizational model of cultural and technological production in the internet age. Evidenced most obviously by mobile telecommunications and social software, the accelerated climate of connection has become so pervasive that it is no longer a novelty to expect constantly accessible information from multiple sources and to consider ourselves perpetually linked with specialized interest communities and environments. Across all practices and disciplines—engineering, geography, economics, media studies, biological sciences, and psychology, to name a few—a rich ecology of technology threatens to overwhelm at the same time that it exhilarates and empowers.

A network is an abstract organizational model, in its broadest sense concerned only with the structure of relationships between things, be they objects or information, which can be applied to the organization of anything from friends lists to genetic algorithms to global military operations. Networks consist classically of nodes, or non-dimensional points of connection, and links, equally non-material connections that usually conform to one of several organizational topologies such as centralized, distributed, bus, or mesh, which effect the nature of the relationships they embody and how they may be analyzed and understood. As a complex energy and material system, what typically qualifies a network are parameters of performance, related to flexibility, self-organization, and adaptability.

Stretching back to the postwar military-industrial momentum of the Rand Corporation in the 1950s, network theory as we understand it today was then—and to a large extent still is—an agglomeration of research from diverse disciplinary backgrounds, including complexity science, mathematics, sociology, and communications theory. In the mid-1990s, however, breakthroughs in the mathematics of complexity teamed with the rapid consumer adoption of telecommunications networks heralded a new phase of network theory and practice involving highly developed communications technologies and the radically altered and to a large degree generationally specific concept of social space that they engendered. This has created a resurgence of interest in the organizational potential of network logics and their applications beyond the internet to the creative fields, which have begun to explore new territories for networks, concerned not with optimized performance but with more humanist parameters involving social organization, aesthetics, and culture.

The implications of contemporary network theory to the creative practitioner has received little attention, however, despite the fact that in an unassuming way, an understanding of connected practices was being established in many disciplines from biology and the mapping of the human genome to the psychology of crowd behavior over the last fifty years.

In 2004 we set out from a broadly defined perspective, inclusive of science, art, and architecture, to explore networks not only through their visible forms but also in terms of operationalizing network theory for its creative potential within design practices. The result was "Distributed Form: Network Practice," a three-day symposium hosted at the College of Environmental Design and the Department of Architecture at the University of California, Berkeley, in October of that year. We conceived of a trajectory of research that would establish a baseline for this moment in design, post-disciplinary in its nature and necessarily as introspective as it is encompassing, that could reformat histories as much as construct new vectors of investigation in a broad range of network forms and their relationship to design in process, practice, and places—what we have called "network practices." As with the symposium, our goal with this book is to analyze how art, science, and architecture shape and are shaped by a diverse array of social, cultural, and technical networks and how they respond to rapidly changing mobile, wireless, and ultimately information-embedded environments.

Our initial intention was to consider notional boundaries of form, which were presently emerging within distributed and networked space. We decided to approach this process as designers of systems and artifacts, manifested through multiple disciplines. But we also came to realize that over time, our interest in networks was not limited to viewing them as a necessary moment in a broader contextualization of the networked society from a design point of view; it was also (and perhaps more importantly) an opportunity for new creative possibility.

With this book, it is our intention to be broadly inclusive. While we run the risk of overextending this discursive field, we also realize that the fundamental structural changes that we face today could not be positioned in any other way than to embrace the pre-condition of the unformed—that is to say, a condition that is yet to be discovered, not fully known, in as much as it could be described as a network-in-formation. Therefore the initial concept of the investigation, "network practices," in turn generated the structure of the book itself, creating a hub from which multiple connections could be established across disciplines, across theory and practice.

We began this research with a question influenced by the sociologist Manuel Castells's *The Rise of the Network Society*: how could we situate the designer within a networked society? To quote Castells, "The network society itself is, in fact, the social structure which is characteristic of what people had been calling for years the information society or post-industrial society."[1] What is the position and responsibility of the designer-as-agent, within this socially based information society? While much work had been done to establish the conditions of the network society, very little had been put into an active frame for creative thinkers across disciplines.

The goal of *Network Practices* is to interrogate these terms in order to provide a substantive and responsive context for design, and particularly for architecture. Clearly networked practices have touched every discipline, every sphere—begging the question, what *isn't* networked? And yet, as ubiquitous as this condition is, there is a significant gap in our collective design knowledge around this issue, one that we hoped to begin to bridge through the development of new strategic thinking.

Designed systems and artifacts are not isolated, but intensifications of more broadly diffused social, technical, and material practices. As designers creating new experiential conditions, we are motivated by a curiosity about new technologies and how they are becoming instantiated within social and cultural phenomena, how they thicken and enrich our relationships, and how they create new cultural conditions and social practices. Castells reminds us that design is never neutral, but plays an active role in creating and maintaining social, technical, and economic networks that process and manage information. We proposed that the symposium should start with the assumption of the network constructed through information technology and then create the opportunity for designers to explain how they were creatively interpreting and responding to the programming of those networks. As the designer's context moves into the sphere of information design, we were interested in capturing the social, cultural, and creative process they also represent.

Beyond technical issues, beyond engineering systems and sensors, our primary ambition is to explore what this new connected environment really means in human terms—in other words to reinforce the notion of a technically enabled humanism within the transformations occurring in information and communication technology. Using this framework we identify certain attractors within larger disciplinary fields, which have thus far gone underexamined:

→ The creative potential of physical, social, and technical networks *in formation*, that create both turbulence and flow, and organize by means of continual adjustments on different scalar levels as a response to changing environmental parameters.

→ The intersection of design, social space, and a range of recently networked media that provide the basis for increasing and changing the nature of our sociability across all scales, creating new opportunities for collaborative practice and a new field of collective media artifacts.

→ Internet and new media art, which affords alternate means of expressions within new media cultural production, as well as advancing open-source software and creative practices, new visual vocabularies and channels for production, and knowledge sharing.

→ Architectural theory and production, which is increasingly being equipped to deal with the complexities of contemporary networked space, developing new forms of practice and exploring new levels of complex spatial conditions and contexts within computational and actual environments.

→ Science, where taping the positive potential of a broader connected ecology and finding new inspiration from complex biological systems is creating both challenges and opportunities for new relationships between design and science.

→ The conceptualization of urbanism as layers of reflexive, contingent, and distributed networks and systems responsive to both far-ranging global and local economic, demographic, and environmental pressures.

The following chapters cannot be neatly organized by these categories, however; rather, each chapter presents a different voice and a different disciplinary interest ranging across many or all of these territories. In this sense, Mark Wigley recognizes not only a historical momentum but a complete reframing of the discipline of architecture itself though network terms. Similarly Michael Speaks captures a sentiment of systemic intelligence that has arisen to challenge traditional easy categorizations of design theory and practice. Christopher Hight presents servo, an architectural practice embodying the potential of networked practice models, while Dagmar Richter explores the spatial potential of networked operations in her studio pedagogy. Peter Bentley mirrors these practices in science through examining the creative potentials of a complex and interconnected understanding of design and biology.

Reframing code as a material practice, open-source programmer and artist C. E. B. Reas addresses the potential of dynamic reactive systems to generate visual compositions. Peter Testa and Devyn Weiser discuss new forms of material agency that include advanced computational methods and digital fabrication processes developed by the Emergent Design Group at MIT under their direction. Within art practice, both David Crawford and George Legrady employ algorithmic processes, albeit very different ones, to uncover intimate and subtle new urban and social territories existing in both media and real space. Crawford employs video as a method of enquiry into contemporary urban practices within the subway, while Legrady's interactive installations and cultural data mappings transform our notions of collective meaning. At a transcontinental scale, the finely grained operations of social and economic forces are expanded by Reinhold Martin's characterization of a networked multinational urbanism.

The richness and breadth of this networked territory, however, demands some further contextualization, which we have attempted both in light of contemporary media theory: relational systems are explored within computational design by Therese Tierney, and through an emerging critical network theory and practice by Anthony Burke.

The purpose of this volume is to cross one media boundary and carry the ideas first voiced at the symposium into a novel context, gaining a different type of gravity as they morph from voice to print. In as much as it is a new trajectory, this volume is also an imperfect and incomplete archive, posing more paths for discussion than we could attempt to resolve. Most importantly, however, this volume attempts to capture the spirit of creative enquiry and enthusiasm that marks a unique moment in design, where crossing disciplines, spatial interactions, and design practices are all poised to be reimagined, moving from one organizational paradigm to the next.

Notes

1...Manuel Castells, *The Information Age: Economy, Society and Culture; Volume 1: The Rise of the Network Society*, 2nd ed. (Malden, MA: Blackwell, 2000).

The Architectural Brain

Mark Wigley

How can we talk about networks and architecture today? Or, how can we not? Silence about networks would be odd. Architects are so immersed in their complex circuitry that we cannot imagine life without them. Yet for the very same reason we cannot really imagine what life is like with them. They are our medium, ever present but invisible, like water to a fish. Perhaps networks only become visible as such in the moments that they fail, and only in the very instant of failure. It is disconnection rather than connection that triggers our perceptions of a system, even a possible debate about it, but the shape of the subject being discussed disappears as quickly as it arrives. Networks are by definition elusively everywhere. Their singular attribute is the self-effacing one of diffusion.

So what does it mean to gather together in a school, a conference, or a book to talk about networks? Why gather in a place to say that every space is now fluidly interlaced with all the others? Why gather to say that we no longer have to gather? Why do the immense distributed networks that we occupy paradoxically require or even produce such dense points of concentration? Rather than tracing the remarkable extension, resilience, and interactivity of our intricate weave of trans-planetary webs, we might do well to think about the points of super-concentration that seem to contradict the diffuse geometry of networks, yet in the end may be their most significant symptom. Instead of thinking about the latest effects of global networks on architecture, we might think about the curious architecture of all networks and the networked condition of all architectures. Perhaps we might even want to consider the thought that architects are network creatures. If the architect is first and foremost a public intellectual, someone who treats the built environment as an articulate and reflective medium, this is a form of network intelligence. Long before any architects talk about networks, the very way they talk, and the effect of the talking, is networked. Indeed, the architect might be nothing more than a visible point of concentration in a less visible network system.

Let's start with a few basic characteristics of a network. Inasmuch as it *is* a network, it is a whole world, a complete spatial system: you cannot simply be inside or outside of it. It is a landscape without an exterior. The operational principle is redundancy. There are always multiple pathways between any two points and multiple options being activated at any one time. Distributed intelligence does not involve an idea moving from one place to another. The network itself is a brain, a thinking machine, and each thought belongs to the network as a whole, regardless of the particular geometry being activated at any moment. Events don't simply happen in the space. The space itself *is* the event.

Such a condition is not new to architecture. While contemporary architectural discourse routinely deploys an edgy network rhetoric of flows, nodes, parallel processing, webs, bandwidth, interfaces, and so on in trying to grasp the unique character of our time, this logic was already incubated in late-seventeenth-century architectural debates through the emergence of a new challenge to the traditional hierarchical understanding of classical theory. In a radical test of the official doctrine, authority started to be found in the inner workings of material and institutional systems rather than in a higher transcendental or political order. This emergent horizontal understanding was diagrammatically embodied in the form of comparative charts, tables, dictionaries, account books, and calculations in which each interconnected entry had equal status. An extended pattern of interconnections defined each situation rather than the things being connected. Architecture could be seen as an agile, responsive, and evolving system like any other to be found in the natural world.

Many different kinds of history can be written of the extended evolution of this horizontal view of architecture, linking Fréart de Chambray's parallel drawings, Claude Perrault's comparative tables, Jean-Nicolas-Louis Durand's graph paper, Gottfried Semper's encyclopedic comparative history, Viollet-le-Duc's anatomical dissections of buildings, Heinrich Wölfflin's pairs of slides, CIAM's standardized analytical grid, Buckminster Fuller's statistics on global resources, and so on. All of these organizational techniques domesticated the field by giving every manifestation of architecture at all locations, scales, periods, and cultures a position in a system and an equivalent status. Such a horizontal system can be entered at any point and traversed in any lateral movement in contrast to the strictly linear trajectory of the hierarchical tradition with its single beginning and end point. A horizontal mentality steadily overhauled the field, reengineering all its operations.

Yet it is crucial to understand that this systems approach remained in an intimate dance with the vertical view that it challenged. It is not by chance that the horizontal understanding emerged at the same time as the first Royal Academies of architecture. In fact, it can be argued that the new institutions were a preemptive defense against it, an allergic reaction that reshaped the dominant hierarchical discourse. The academies tried to establish a synergy between royal and transcendental authority by defending and enforcing the classical ideal that the beauty and power of architecture derives from the cosmic resonance of its proportions with the eternal harmonies of the universe—such that the well-proportioned building could act as a privileged bridge between the imperfect transitory physical world and the perfect higher world of timeless ideas. But the newly official academic doctrine, as lectured and published by François Blondel, the first head of the first Royal Academy in

Paris, was promptly challenged by the writings of Claude Perrault, who imitated the methods of contemporary scientists by simply measuring all the columns said to be beautiful and noting that they do not correspond to the rules dictated in the classical treatises, nor with each other. The argument kept going back and forth through subsequent generations of theorists, with the official hierarchical account of architecture stubbornly resisting the systems account but being increasingly defined only by its resistance and ultimately being subordinated to the view that it was countering. The academy had the power over the discipline but was forever on defense, continually scrambling to make adjustments to its declarations and negotiate finer points of interpretation of existing buildings, archeological remains, new designs, and texts. Meanwhile, an extended lineage of theorists deployed a comparative logic to transform architecture into a system composed of interlocking and equally valued elements, operating as a kind of biological mechanism, and evolving on many fronts. Architectural discourse itself became an organism that could move sideways. No longer standing still, looking up and obeying timeless orders, the discourse fixed its eye on the horizon and started to explore an ever-widening territory.

Closely linked to the evolution of modern science and industrialization, this systems approach would become a manifesto for twentieth-century architecture. Despite all the heterogeneous symptoms of so-called "modern" architecture, it can be argued that its central polemic was simply the attempt to make the horizontal understanding concrete. Modern architecture is in every way horizontal. Not just in the canonic horizontality of the roof and windows reinforced by the apparent disengagement from the ground (although these were precisely meant to displace the hierarchical tradition) but by the horizontality of the system itself: the socialist ambitions of the political model; the mass distribution of a mass-produced array of elements with the same status; and a new freedom to laterally redistribute people, objects, buildings, and activities. The techniques for classifying, organizing, and even rationalizing architecture became the actual form of the architecture—such that even a trained decorative artist like Le Corbusier could starkly assert in 1925 that beauty is classification and present the Roneo filing cabinet as the idealized tool of his time: "*it is necessary to have a file on the filing system itself....*This new system of filing which clarifies our needs, has an effect on the lay-out of rooms, and of buildings."[1]

Such a horizontal understanding was first explicit in city planning, as the discipline devoted to the establishment of infrastructural systems for distributing objects across a field and regulating overlapping flows at different scales. Cities are parallel processing machines. They can only be networks. Buildings are traditionally understood as non-horizontal elements positioned within a flat network, singular events within the framework of a communication system. But in the twentieth century, the horizontal network logic of overlapping infrastructural communication systems made its way into the buildings themselves. Interiors became circuits. Flow on the outside ever more seamlessly merged into flow on the inside until the line defining the limit of the building became paper thin. This digestion of the network

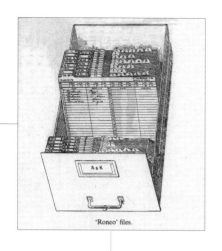

'Roneo' files.

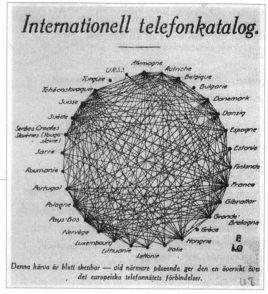

Internationell telefonkatalog.

Denna härva är blott skenbar — vid närmare påseende ger den en översikt över det europeiska telefonnätets förbindelser.

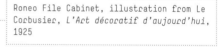

Roneo File Cabinet, illustration from Le Corbusier, *L'Art décoratif d'aujourd'hui*, 1925

International Telephone Network. From Le Corbusier's file cabinet collection of material for *L'Esprit Nouveau*

"Regrouping around cooperative centers," illustration from Le Corbusier, *Les trois établissements humains*, 1945

Le Corbusier, Venice Hospital project, 1964

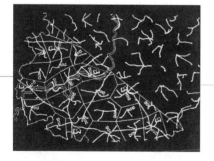

took time, even with the role models like Le Corbusier, who so literally brought the flows of movement of the outside into his buildings by staging a smooth transition from plane to car to promenading occupant to mobile furniture. In the early 1920s, for example, he was collecting images of the dense weave of international telephone networks, but the only time he applied the word "network" to what he was designing was with his traffic patterns, as in the Radiant City scheme of 1933. By the mid-1940s, with *The Three Human Establishments*, he was envisaging more complex forms of interlocking distributed networks. The sense of architecture defined by enclosing walls gave way to that of the extended field of communication. And late works like the Venice Hospital project of 1964 removed any distinction between building and network by monumentalizing a single infrastructural weave—realizing the potential of inhabited infrastructure already envisaged in the horizontal skyscraper projects for Algiers and Rio. The communication system becomes the only occupiable object. The idea of a closed architecture gives way to that of an interlaced field without limits. The free plan's challenge to walls that turned the interior into a landscape of movement now turned the exterior landscape of movement into an interior.

For many modern architects it was the orthogonal grid itself that acted as the paradigm of the open non-hierarchical horizontal system extending infinitely outward across the landscape and inward through modular units at ever-smaller scales. But this relentlessly horizontal system is still marked by barriers between inside and outside, even if the barriers have been radically thinned down and perforated. The grid is just a supportive infrastructure for staging spaces. The network is that which allows things to work but is not the work itself. Buildings, people, activities, and events still occur *in* and *on* rather than *as* the net.

It was after World War II that horizontally distributed infrastructure polemically became the work itself. Architecture is no longer the positioning of objects in a field; the field itself becomes a kind of object. Rather than moving through a system to reach a static enclosure or building, you never leave the movement system. The paradigmatic image for this wide-ranging effort was Louis Kahn's 1951–53 plan of Philadelphia built out of a dense network of little arrows, forming a set of agitated dotted lines, a weave of flows like an electric circuit. This horizontal weave is literally extended upward in a three-dimensional weave to form the City Center tower Kahn designed in collaboration with Ann Tyng. The diffuse tower displaces the sense of walls with its corrugated form but is limited by its fixed floors. The mesh ultimately acts as a cage for suspending a more traditional understanding of space. Konrad Wachsmann went one step further in the same years by presenting vast space frame hangars in which the space inside the frame itself was bigger, and more influential in the discipline, than the massive space it covered. Buckminster Fuller's 1958 space frame exhibited at the Museum of Modern Art in New York tried to go even further by removing by the floor along with any simple opposition between horizontal and vertical. Fuller devoted his career to modeling such three-dimensional networks and testing new ways of occupying them. Likewise, Yona Friedman and

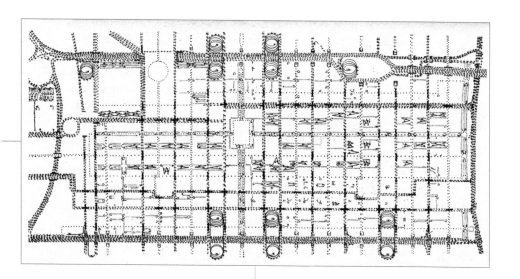

Louis Kahn, Philadelphia Traffic Study,
1953

Konrad Wachsmann, Airline Hangar project,
1953

Eduard Shultze-Fielitz designed the kit-set frameworks for hovering cities in which people would live suspended inside the infrastructure. International architectural magazines filled up with images of structural systems that could be assembled to form ever-larger buildings, vast landscapes of interconnected nodes.

All this extended research on space frame architecture can be understood as an unconscious attempt to visibly model the invisible electronic networks that increasingly defined contemporary life. In the same way that the classical architect makes visible the hidden geometry of the universe, the postwar architect makes visible the hidden geometry of electronics. Life is literally seen to be nurtured by a circuitry of energized webs. The unresolved question of how such network structures could be occupied echoed the unresolved question of our basic relationship with electronics.

Fuller repeatedly positioned himself within his geodesic space frames, as in a *Life* magazine postcard showing him suspended in the 1958 MoMA frame. The image is an invitation to join him in the web. Anyone could live there. He tries to look as ordinary as possible, having decided early on that in order to be trusted, he had to look boring. He did a study of the look of every worker, concluded that bank clerks were the dullest looking, and carefully modeled his look after them. These images say even the most boring person can live within this new kind of frame. Yet such a space frame operating as a kind of jungle-gym is still a more or less traditional definition of space. You don't live in the web itself in most of these projects but in the space it frames. The projects only offer a more sophisticated version of the kind of freedom offered by the horizontal grid.

The key development in network architecture occurred when network structures were developed in which the force, freedom, and beauty were in the network itself, with the inhabitants occupying the nodes and links themselves. In the three-dimensional webs of Archigram's Ron Herron, Peter Cook, and Dennis Crompton, for example, you never leave the structure of the web. When the space suit, space craft, and space station are the architectural models, it is understood that to leave the system is to die. One lives inside the plumbing. In this extended lineage of design from Fuller through Wachsmann, Archigram, Archizoom, and Superstudio, there is always a computer driving the environment—monitoring, maintaining, responding. Architects are trying to draw a life in which everything is computerized. The architecture itself is animated by electronics or even visualized as electronic, most obviously in Crompton's 1963 Computer City: A Synthesized Metropolis with Electronic Changeability, which represents the interactive software system for a responsive city as if people literally live in the circuitry itself. The extended network landscape in which the projects were built were understood as circuits, even modeled with electric wires, as in Archigram's Plug-In City Network, where the landscape of Britain is effectively turned into a circuit board. Images of circuit boards often appeared in architectural magazines, books, catalogs, and exhibitions, floating without explanation as inspirational icons alongside projects, geometric figures

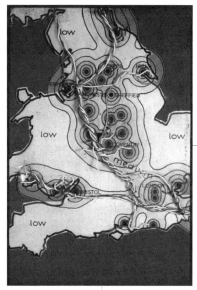

Archigram, Plug-In City Network, 1964

Buckminster Fuller in his 1958 MoMA space frame

Dennis Crompton, Computer City project, 1964

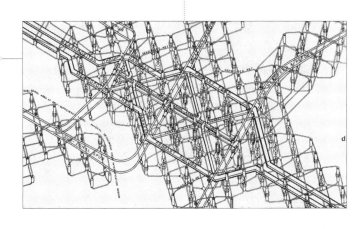

to be treated with the same reverence as classical columns or the human body as the new role model. As Serge Chermayeff and Christopher Alexander noted alongside one of these full-page images in 1963: "The sophisticated organization of the printed TV circuit, for example, is totally unmatched by the organization of the dwelling that contains it."[2] Architecture dreams of becoming a circuit board.

In the end, it is the horizontality of these schemes of the late 1950s and 1960s that gives them the key weblike quality. While the space frame supposedly defeats any simple opposition between up and down, left and right, or forward and backward to liberate any desired trajectory, it is the lateral movement that becomes polemical. Network culture is by definition multidimensional, but connectivity is primarily visualized as horizontal. The internet, for example, is seen as a lateral system—wide rather than deep. Not by chance was "WorldWideWeb" the label coined in 1990 for the first internet browser. After thousands of years of horizontal networks, like shipping lanes, all traffic, all forms of flow, are understood to be horizontal. Despite all Fuller's efforts to visualize outer space as the sea of the future (as in his 1969 essay "Vertical is to Live, Horizontal is to Die"),[3] the planet is experienced as a fixed horizontal plane rather than a high-velocity spinning sphere. Connectivity at any scale is seen to be lateral. It is the horizontality of the circuit board that allows it to act as an icon, and it is in constructing the image of a horizontal world that architects visualize contemporary conditions.

This horizontal image takes a while to evolve. Early projects, like Kahn's Philadelphia scheme, with light horizontal webs sprouting heavier towers, give way to schemes like Alison and Peter Smithson's 1958 Hauptstadt plan for Berlin, where the sculptural effect of the horizontal communication weave is emphasized more than the buildings it supports. These in turn give way to schemes where the weave is thickened up to become the building itself, which Alison Smithson retrospectively labeled as a tradition of "mat buildings." The decade or so from Aldo van Eyck's Orphanage to Le Corbusier's Venice Hospital is rich with projects for a horizontal sandwich in which diverse overlapping lateral movements are always possible at any location. Horizontality knows no limit, from the orphanage to George Candilis and Shadrach Woods' university campus to Yona Friedman's city to Piet Blom's woven region to Constant's planetary-sized New Babylon. By definition, even the smallest example of a network building carries the potential to be extended infinitely. It is the absence of horizontal constraint that defines this work. These projects are essays in extension. Finally then, the network as the world, one building at the size of the planet, an infrastructural weave extending beyond every horizon—flattened into a relentless "furnished parking lot" in Archizoom's No-Stop City of 1970, and perfected in Superstudio's Supersurface of 1972, a pure horizontal densely packed with the circuitry needed to sustain interactive life and spreading itself across every landscape. With a single stretched circuit board as the stage for global life, architecture as sheltering interior is finally displaced by architecture as the fully exposed horizontal, with people nomadically wandering across "earth, rendered homogenous

Illustration from Chermayeff and
Alexander, *Community and Privacy*, 1963

Superstudio, Supersurface project, 1972

Archizoom, No-Stop City project, 1970

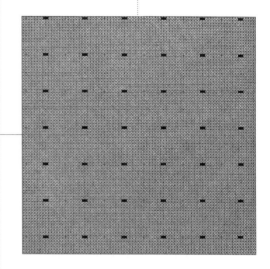

through an energy and information grid…a network of energy and information extending to every properly inhabitable area…without protective walls"—horizontal drift as the endpoint of network architecture.[4]

All this polemical horizontality is linked to a concept of freedom. In the same way that there was a crude association between the horizontal logic of the 1920s buildings and the political project for a more egalitarian distribution of social and material resources, there is an association between the ever-expanding lateral networks of the 1960s and a kind of participatory democracy with expressions of individual creativity. Constant, an artist inspired as much by Fuller, van Eyck, the Smithsons, and Wachsmann as by his dissident surrealist colleagues in the Situationist International, defines his 1956–74 city of the near future as a "wide world web" for spontaneous play.[5] All the technical infrastructure is buried below the surface so that the open framework above can be endlessly reconfigured. The network is not just a space of free movement but a freedom to invent whole new kinds of movement. The vast sprawling scaffolding that defines the new city is intended as a postrevolutionary incubator for new kinds of spatial practice.

The most sophisticated version of such a network incubator is Cedric Price's Fun Palace project of 1961–64. It was envisioned sitting on the banks of the Thames River in London as a vast open scaffolding. Looking more closely, we can see different event spaces suspended within it—scaffoldings within scaffoldings, as with Constant's New Babylon. The logic of the project is again that the people occupying the space determine what is happening and thereby redetermine the architecture. The space is continually reshaped by the changing desires of the inhabitants; with up to 55,000 at any one time, there is a continual flux as events and the interconnections between them evolve. There are no walls or roof, just a plinth below which all the technical systems are housed and above which the open scaffolding is topped by a huge gantry crane moving backward and forward when needed. It's like the horizontal plane of a theatrical stage surrounded by the machinery for moving sets around and adjusting the atmosphere of sound, light, and information for a performance. The open grid of towers houses elevators and continuously necessary equipment like bathrooms, but such units are clipped on so that they can be moved. Everything in between the towers, including the rotating escalators, moves in response to visitor demands. The temporary occupants are at once actors on a stage and collaborative directors.

It is all very thin—so light that there is almost nothing there. In the first image published of Fun Palace in 1964, showing a typical slice of the building, you can see that the actual structure has almost disappeared. What is drawn more heavily is the activity spaces, yet even these spaces are trying not to be rooms but zones of a certain atmospheric intensity. Fun Palace is intended to be a kind of incubator for new kinds of nomadic architecture that refuse to be fixed. No major event space is allowed to last for more than seven days and all the small spaces are meant to turn over two or three times a day. It is a huge building trying not to be a building. No walls, roof, doors, or windows; just a series of temporary architectures with each

Cedric Price, Fun Palace project, 1964

Fun Palace, illustration from *New Scientist*, May 1964

Fun Palace, illustration from *The Architectural Review*, January 1965

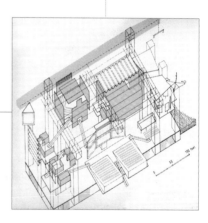

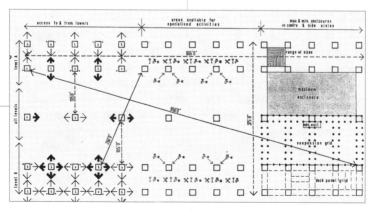

trying to be less visible than the events occurring within them, the contributions of the visitors being more decisive than that of the architect. The logic of the project is established in an early drawing of the three-dimensional grid which will act as the basic territory for experimentation. But this net is not fetishized. It will never appear as such. The whole project is a kind of dotted line, a ghostly absence of a distinct form in which building elements will be temporarily suspended. Architecture has to withdraw, as it were, in order that dynamic networks can be activated.

Fun Palace is a network incubator. While Price positions the project in the midst of a dense array of overlapping streams of transportation and information, he doesn't so much build the image of a network as an image of the possibility of assembling networks on an intimate and daily basis. The key details are not those of the scaffolding but of the atmospheric zones of "intensity." The black squares in the middle are the three big fixed towers that make it possible for these fluid zones of connectivity to be established above the horizontal floor—in yet another example of a diffuse network being made possible by points of super-concentration. The most important drawing of the project, a <u>calculation of the key dimensions</u>, contains all the information for the building at all its levels. It is a calculation of proportions, no longer the classical proportions articulating an eternal immaterial order, but the proportions with the greatest productivity for generating the maximum number and variety of material exchanges. The argument being made is that if you had to make a machine that can generate and sustain the maximum number and variety of social networks, this would be it. So a new network architecture emerges, a delicate ghostlike trace that operates more as landscape than building.

This project is a test tube for network thinking. It is truly modern in the sense of being an attempt to go beyond the free plan to produce a free four-dimensional volume. Again it presupposes the complete integration of electronic circuitry, software, structure, and activity. The whole project is conceived as a series of feedback loops. Price formed a Cybernetics Committee dedicated to figuring out the interactive system by which information would be digested and translated into strategic decisions about activities. Gordon Pask, a prominent cybernetic theorist, directed the committee and detailed the kind of circuitry needed to allow the system to continuously evolve. Price did a preliminary survey with questionnaires to visualize the kind of desires being responded to. He looked for likely activity patterns and tabulated the results into "affinity" charts that map the hidden associations between one kind of activity and another, so that the design could maximize the interconnections and minimize interferences between sequences and juxtapositions of activities.

The whole interactive system was understood as an education machine, a "university of the streets," as Joan Littlewood, the client and originator of the Fun Palace idea, described it.[6] The structure conflated science and entertainment to enable working-class people to educate themselves by following their own desires. This strategy was extended in Price's 1965 Potteries Thinkbelt project for a new kind of university, where innovative forms of knowledge exchange are made possible by establishing intense temporary nodes in a regional network. Nodes between existing rail and air links were to be supplemented by new kinds of links and a set of "electronic audio-visual exchange points" distributed across the landscape to create a "largely invisible network related to communication, information and learning."[7] An architecture that thinks, the Thinkbelt is designed as a form of circuitry where again points of concentration sustain new forms of flow and a flickering horizontal web is activated as a kind of inhabitable computer. Price tries to shape a new form of intelligence by de-powering traditional architectural mechanisms. Shelter gives way to the modulation of flow. What remains of a building is a provisional node in a thinking machine.

These architects are not only producing images of the network world we are living in. They are also producing images of their own modes of operation. More than designs for structures operating as open-ended networking machines that represent the extent to which architecture can integrate itself with electronic systems to incubate new mutating forms of connectivity by giving up its classical functions of stability and security, these are also images of the way architecture thinks.

Take Candilis and Woods' Berlin Free University project of 1964, the most celebrated of the horizontal "groundscrapers." It is conceived of as a thinking machine—not a mechanism within which thinking occurs but a mechanism that produces thinking by mixing diverse forms of knowledge. The architects' diagram of "the idea of university" shows a network of overlapping dotted lines mixing different forms of "special information" to produce "general information" once the usual built barriers to exchange are removed. The concept is all too familiar to architects since it was built into the architectural discipline from the start, when Vitruvius insisted that the unique characteristic of the architect is the need to be familiar with all the other specialized areas of knowledge. Architecture is seen to lie at the intersection of ideas. Any particular design requires the architect to resolve many seemingly incompatible forces. The architect is seen as a form of synthetic intelligence. Design is understood as a form of thinking and the space of the architect's studio is a space of pure thinking. This approach organizes architectural education, with each design studio seen as a group of people networked together in a complex pattern to address a complex problem. These studios are in turn networked together to form schools that are networked to each other in numerous ways to form an international web for architectural thinking that is interlaced with that of the profession. The result is a vast interlocked set of spaces for synthetic thinking, a thinking machine. The buildings produced by the profession are more the products of this network than the individual designers with which they are associated. In a sense, the buildings act as a set of loudspeakers for monitoring the ongoing reflections by the architectural net. The subtle blurring of inside and outside in the Free University's potentially endless web that fosters lateral exchanges, so that the institution can think itself through questions that by definition lack limits, turns the architect's unique form of knowledge into a physical instrument.

This merging of intelligent architecture and architectural intelligence is clearest in the work of Konrad Wachsmann, the apprentice of the Expressionist Hans Poelzig, who built Albert Einstein's summer house in 1929, escaped to the United States during the war, and became the ultimate network man. Having exemplified the systems approach in his 1941–42 collaboration with Walter Gropius on the General Panel System Packaged House, in which factory-made interlocking parts could be "knotted" together on site with a novel form of connector that made no distinction between horizontal and vertical linkage,[8] he became director of Advanced Building Research at the Institute of Design in Chicago in 1951. His position was dependent on bringing in sponsored research, and he immediately worked with students on a project commissioned by the Air Force to design the vast aircraft hangars that would be so influential when published internationally. In the winter of 1953 he collaborated with the students again to produce the ultimate architectural web design with the development of a unique jointing system. It is the definitive web because the lines that form it are twisted around each other to form the connections. There is no distinction between link and node. The sense of coherent structure is again produced by a kind of knot. In a sense, the whole system is a single endless loose knot. It is the most extreme case of Wachsmann's attempts to produce "free space" by undermining the idea of "solid structure" in favor of a "porous character."[9] While this subtle and sophisticated system allows for infinite extension in all directions, the canonic renderings symptomatically emphasize the sense of horizontal extension. Wachsmann was giving the most precise technical form to the horizontal ambition of twentieth-century architecture.

It is not by chance that such web designs emerge from collaborative work in the context of education. The network intelligence of a school of architecture is used to produce images of network intelligence—medium becoming message becoming medium. Wachsmann was convinced that architectural education had to take the form of experimental research in an age in which "it is no longer possible simply to communicate a precise body of knowledge founded on a rigid status quo" and "areas of study are expanding considerably."[10] New structures of architectural education have to be designed to both respond to this expansion and accelerate it, a new kind of curriculum and a new kind of laboratory. In 1959, Wachsmann echoed his precise drawings of the efficient factory organization for the production of the Packaged House in his diagrams for the educational organization used in the Advanced Building Research unit in Chicago where sets of three students are networked together in a series of knots so that up to twenty-one students can collaborate to solve a design problem. Even the layout of the room is prescribed with a grid of worktables for each set of three students, culminating in a larger table for discussion to foster direct interaction between all team members, surrounded by a "cluster" of four drawing boards to continuously monitor the evolution of their thinking.

This diagram of a factory for thinking was again put into operation when Wachsmann moved to California in 1964 to run the Institute of Building Research at

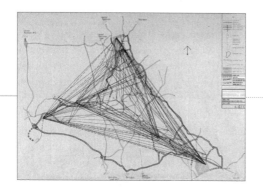

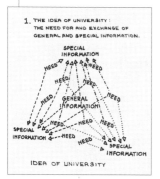

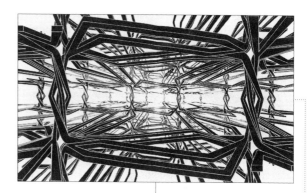

Konrad Waschsmann, Experimental
Structural Web, 1953

Shadrach Woods, diagram for Berlin Free
University project, 1964

Cedric Price, Potteries Thinkbelt
project, primary road network, 1966

Konrad Waschsmann, interlocking
organization of design studio teams, 1959

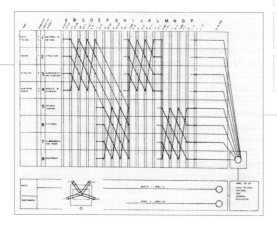

USC, instituting a network approach to architectural education. Three years later, he added another kind of drawing in his "Programming Guide," a study of his own program sponsored by the Graham Foundation. He argued that the whole point of the program was to displace the concept of the master with that of the "master team," describing his ideal school as "an interdisciplinary system without the barriers of faculty specialization, exploding in universal, international and comprehensive planned research."[11] It is the word "exploding" that is so important. These are not just happy families networking under the Californian sun but the incubation of explosively radical innovations. Wachsmann drew the "organism" of his Institute of Building Research just as he drew his building structures. What you see is a more or less standard multidimensional network. No longer the hierarchical synthesis of Gropius's diagram of the Bauhaus curriculum as a series of concentric rings around a core. No center, top, bottom, or sides. The six parts of the Institute (library, teacher training, research testing, faculty, graduate studies, educational studies) spin around each other with equal weight, and each in turn is made up of six parts that are themselves made up of six parts. A drawing of what Wachsmann calls the "unlimited expansion of any given problem or task simultaneously reaching in all directions," entitled "spatial expansion of categories of facts, subject matters and relations" shows how such a system is designed to explode outward, without limit.[12] And a final drawing shows how the Institute of Building Research explodes out to connect with the other parts of the university, which in turn explodes out into the world. The design of education, like the design of a networked space frame, is the design of a knot that simultaneously reaches inward and outward, a twist that concentrates the forces in a set of isolated points so that they can flow.

It is not just that the drawings of the educational network resemble those of the structural systems designed to articulate new forms of movement. In reverse, the structural systems are also images of the discipline. The new drawings of interwoven structural webs are a kind of self-reflection upon the field. They are a refining of the machinery with which architects think, or, more precisely, the machinery itself that thinks and produces architects as a kind of a side effect, a visible node concentrating an invisible array of invisible flows.

This radical thinking through of networks, associating the brain of the architect, the school, the building, and the city, is linked to the idea of the prosthetic extension of the human body through electronics, most famously in the contemporary work of Marshall McLuhan, who argued so relentlessly that one of the consequences of our electronic connection to globalized networks of communication is that we have lost the simple boundary of our body, that our bodies have been expanded to the size of the planet, and are therefore irreducibly social. In other words, social life is not one body coming into contact with another. Rather, we share one hyper-interconnected body. Our internal nerves are continuous with those of computers. People are wired into thinking machines, and this planetary-sized body is a single brain. In *The Gutenberg Galaxy* of 1962, for example, McLuhan refers to the "new organic-biological modes of the electronic world." Electronics is biological in character: "the world has become a computer, an electronic brain…and as our sensors have gone outside us, Big Brother goes inside."[13] Prosthetic extension is paralleled by extension inward, with electronics going as deeply into consciousness as consciousness has reached outwards. In *The Medium is the Massage* of 1967 McLuhan offers an image of webbed stockings to illustrate "When information rubs against information…"[14] What is the implication? The body becomes the network and the network becomes a sensuous body. When networks rub together, when information is brushed against information, you get something of the pleasure normally associated with bodies. The medium is literally the massage. McLuhan likewise uses an image of the woven pattern of a computer circuit board opposite the head of a child as the image of what it is to educate. Again, the images of brain, body, computer, and school become one. The prosthetic extension of human nerves into ever larger circuits defines network space.

There is a long history to this conflation of images. Nerves have been a big theme in twentieth-century architecture, and were literally pictured in anatomical images of the nerves of the architect's idealized client offered, for example, by Le Corbusier in 1925 and Friedrich Kiesler in 1938. Such images of the internal wiring of the human body are juxtaposed with images of the first circuits with electronic valves in the 1940s, and from around 1964 on they will symptomatically be replaced by images of the wiring of computers. The discussion of computer networks arises as a direct continuation of the discussion of the nervous system.

Architects like Richard Neutra were obsessed with nerves and how the inner nerves of the body might deal with the outside, and how the outer nerves provided by technological systems might reconfigure the body and mind. In imagining the built environment as "an organically possible extension of ourselves," he argued in 1954 that the designer "deals primarily with nervous systems, and he caters to them. He may well contemplate with awe and interest the huge number of the in-bringing, nerve fibers—half a million of them."[15] Fuller had argued since the late 1930s that technology was an extension of the human nervous system. Every tool, from "simple lever" to "electronic tube," was an "organic" and "evolutionary" step toward a "new species," as he put it in a 1940 essay on industrialization for *Fortune*.[16] By the early 1960s, he was arguing that all schools of architecture needed to network themselves together since industrialization had prosthetically extended all the senses of the body to produce "a total world-encircling network organism… a self-correcting, nervous intelligence"[17] that could only be responded to by adopting the comprehensive integrative systems logic of the human brain that it echoed, rather than traditional forms of specialized knowledge.

Kiesler had offered one of the most extended explorations of the issue when working on "extended senses," such as in his "Vision Machine" drawings from around 1938–42. He is just trying to visualize the perception of an object by a body in a room, but the nerve which is doing the looking is drawn strongly and the body is fading away into a ghostly outline, with something like the brain being all that remains. The nerves are

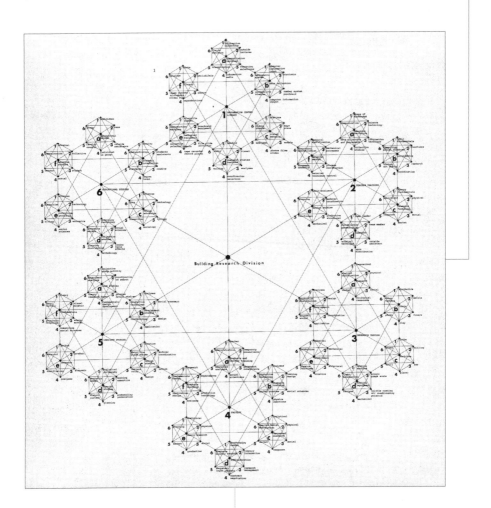

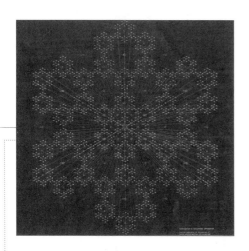

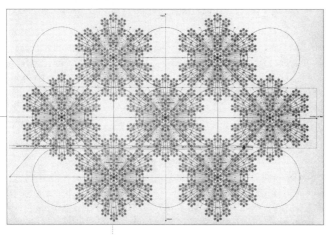

Konrad Waschsmann, University
Organization, 1965

Konrad Waschsmann, "Spatial expansion of
categories of facts, subject matters and
relations," 1965

Konrad Waschsmann, Building Research
Division organization, 1965

"What happens when information rubs
against information...," Marshall McLuhan,
The Medium is the Massage, 1967

directly passing from the inside to the outside, unblocked by the outer limits of the body or the limits of the room. Body and room are displaced by an electrical system, a circuit. Like many of his colleagues, Kiesler repeatedly insisted that architecture is itself a species with a nervous system to be wired into that of its occupants.

Kiesler accelerated his vision machine research when running the Laboratory for Design Correlation at Columbia University from 1937–42. As with the network architects—Fuller, Wachsmann, Woods, and Price—who likewise elaborated detailed theories of education and used the word "laboratory" to describe their ideal teaching space, Kiesler made a direct association between the organization of the designs produced, their intended educational effect, and the organization of the teaching machine that produces them. When publishing a project done in collaboration with the students at the lab in *Architectural Record*, Kiesler again insisted on nerves and prosthetics. His collaborative research studio, like those of Denise Scott-Brown and Rem Koolhaas decades later, depended on network thinking, both in the object designed (a book storage system seen as a flexible node in the flow of information) and in the collaborative strategies deployed. The text argues that we live in a technological world made up of tools that have extended the body out, in addition to the natural and social world. And the world of tools keeps expanding. Biological science is the model. Kiesler offers a Darwinian account of the evolution of tools, insisting that "*technology itself follows laws of hereditary in its own development.*"[18] So technology evolves according to genetic laws, and Kiesler offers a diagram of how new standard types emerge from productive mutations.

This radical blurring of psychology, biology, and technology—"psycho-physiological" or "bio-technical" in Kiesler's terms—echoes nineteenth-century debates occurring at the time Darwin formulated his ideas on evolution that can be traced within the thinking of Le Corbusier in the 1920s, Fuller in the 1930s, and up through McLuhan and the experimental architects of the 1960s and early 1970s, such that Superstudio can matter-of-factly describe the computerization of their project for the ultimate horizontal Supersurface in terms of the way "tools extend the human body."[19] When Superstudio joined the long list of network architects elaborating detailed theories of education—describing the displacement of the traditional university when "every point on the earth's surface is connected up to the network of computers" feeding their project[20]—they were simply completing a nineteenth-century argument about prosthetics that had been steadily reorganizing architectural discourse. The key development was the gradual shift from nerves through electricity to electronics, and Kiesler is right on the cusp of this shift. When presenting the book-storage system, he argues that everything inside the body and outside it is "electromagnetic." While isolating the nerves and discarding the fleshy body, he keeps his eye on television, imagining its replacement of the book and its effects on the experience of objects even before it has really arrived.

Such seeds of much of contemporary thinking about electronics in architecture can already be found in modern architecture's reflections on electricity, traffic,

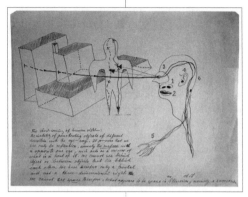

Illustration from John Entenza, "What is a House?" *Arts and Architecture*, July 1944

Friedrich Kiesler, "Extended Senses," 1938-1942

Friedrich Kiesler, Morphology-Chart, *Architectural Record*, September 1939

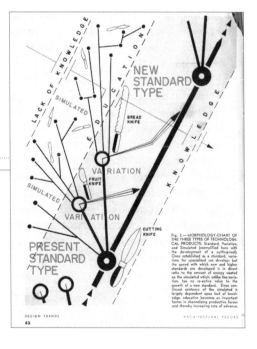

organization, and communication, but it is in the hands of McLuhan—deeply influenced by the architectural voices of Buckminster Fuller, Sigfried Giedion, and Jaqueline Tyrwhitt—that the transition from nerves to electronics is finally established. It is McLuhan who makes the final step to visualize humans in completely electronic terms, reclassifying the human as an electronic species, such that the architectural responsibility to house humanity became a responsibility to shape flows of information. The design of shelters turns into the design of networks and the laboratory for our current explorations of digital architecture was installed.

What I am offering here is just a sketch of the kinds of argument that have over a very long time set up the conditions for today's fast-track experiments with networks in architecture schools. But if architectural discourse is dominated by thinking about networks, and has been for an extended time, and is itself a networked way of thinking—a machine for thinking, a computer—and if the architect is a side effect or concentration in this intelligent system, a form of distributed intelligence, then what does this intelligence try to do? What is all the thinking ultimately about? How does the architectural brain think? What does it do with its intelligence?

We shouldn't assume that this disciplinary brain of ours is creative in the sense of the spontaneous production of novel formulations. It could more convincingly be argued that the mechanism is designed to minimize the amount of novel formulations, the best ideas occurring in spite of the system. The human brain, like any other organ, is designed for survival. Its purpose is to ensure the safe passage of genetic information to the next generation. Almost all of its operations are designed to ensure that nothing happens, with rare innovations, spontaneous mutations, providing a kind of defense against a changing environment. Likewise, the architectural brain is devoted to the survival of the architect as a species and achieves its goal by minimizing innovation but not entirely suppressing it. If the basic principle of all networks is redundancy, most architectural discourse is polemically redundant. Our discipline is as defensive a system as it is possible to imagine. It is calculated to slow things down and distribute resources so evenly to minimize significant events. The global infrastructure of professional organizations, schools, magazines, books, conferences, and lectures is an array of concentrated nodes that safely redistributes and diffuses energy throughout the network. More than a million architecture students around the world are efficiently networked to each other to slow things down. The discipline provides shelter by minimizing surprise.

Most of our discourse is devoted to absorbing innovation, but every now and then there is a productive mutation. We are products of the very long architectural project to establish a form of horizontal mobility. We are embedded within an intelligent web as parts of an architectural brain, but are hopefully trying to look beyond the horizon that has been so patiently assembled—gathering our thoughts here before jumping over the edge.

Notes

....

1...Le Corbusier, *The Decorative Art of Today*, trans. James I. Dunnett (Cambridge: MIT Press, 1987), 77.

2...Serge Chermayeff and Christopher Alexander, *Community and Privacy: Towards a New Architecture of Humanism* (New York: Doubleday, 1963), 196.

3...Buckminster Fuller, "Vertical is to Live, Horizontal is to Die," *American Scholar* 39, no. 1 (Winter 1969–70).

4...Superstudio, "Life or the Public Image of Truly Modern Architecture," *Casabella* 367 (July 1973): 15–27.

5...See Mark Wigley, *The Hyper-Architecture of Desire: Constant's New Babylon* (Rotterdam: 010, 1998).

6...Joan Littlewood, "A Laboratory of Fun," *New Scientist* 38 (May 14, 1964): 432–33.

7...Cedric Price, "Life Conditioning," *Architectural Design* 36 (October 1966): 483–94.

8...Konrad Wachsmann and Walter Gropius, "House in 'Industry': A System for the Manufacture of Industrialized Building Elements," *Arts and Architecture* (May 1947): 28–34.

9...Konrad Wachsmann, *The Turning Point of Building*, trans. Thomas E. Burton (New York: Reinhold, 1961), 231.

10...Ibid., 202.

11...Konrad Wachsmann, *Programming Guide* (Los Angeles: Building Research Institute, School of Architecture, University of Southern California, 1965). Summarized in Konrad Wachsmann, "Research: The Mother of Invention," *Arts and Architecture* (April 1967).

12...Ibid.

13...Marshall McLuhan, *The Gutenberg Galaxy* (Toronto: University of Toronto Press, 1962), 32.

14...Marshall McLuhan, *The Medium is the Massage*, (New York: Bantam Books, 1967).

15...Richard Neutra, *Survival Through Design* (New York: Oxford University Press, 1954), 21 and 197.

16...Buckminster Fuller, "U.S. Industrialization," *Fortune* 21, no. 2 (1940).

17...Buckminster Fuller, "New Forms vs. Reforms: Letter to the World Architectural Students," in John McHale, ed., *Document 1: World Design Science Decade 1965–1975, Phase 1* (Carbondale: Southern Illinois University, 1963), 57.

18...Friedrich Kiesler, "On Correalism and Biotechnique: A Definition and a New Approach to Building Design," *Architectural Record* (Sept. 1939): 60–75.

19...Superstudio, "Life or the Public Image of Truly Modern Architecture," 22.

20...Superstudio, "Education," *Casabella* 368–369 (Aug.–Sept. 1973): 100–04.

Redefining Network Paradigms

Anthony Burke

There is no finality in architecture—only continuous change.
—Walter Gropius

Never believe that a smooth space will suffice to save us.
—Gilles Deleuze and Félix Guattari

New Nets: Old Visions

In a way, the visions of the 1960s have become a reality. As Archigram and Superstudio among others anticipated, we plug in, turn on, and tune up our environment. We are global nomads untethered in an ocean of access, floating in the flux of information and capital that creates the background of our happily networked and connected lives. The enabling infrastructures of communication and data networks that were fantasized in the early modern '30s, engineered in the thermonuclear paranoia of the '50s, and politicized and socialized in the counter-culture of the '60s and '70s, are now materialized, bureaucratized, and commercialized as the ubiquitous organizing structure for the post-consumer[1] dynamics of Empire.[2]

However, now that we are here, the resemblance is only superficial to the technologically enhanced and connected futures imagined forty-five years ago. In the broadest technological, political, philosophical, social, and biological sense, network structures have become not the alternative to, but the dominant structure of power in the third era of modernism. Networks are the *modus operandi* of bureaucracies and corporations as much as environmental resistance groups and terrorist cells. Control, not freedom, has become absolutely distributed, and while we enjoy unprecedented access to information and personal communications devices, we are simultaneously smothered by the cloying ubiquity of networks that have no outside, while our media is characterized as "the most highly controlled mass media hitherto known."[3] In the short time since Archigram's first projects, network technologies that motivated visions like Constant Nieuwenhuis's *New Babylon* have moved from the polemics of the visual to the ambience of the infrastructural.

As tempting as it is to read today's networks as realizations of the various visions of networks employed throughout twentieth-century modernism, they are

Security camera, part of a surveillance
network installed during the most recent
restoration at Le Corbusier's Villa Savoy

Diagram of network connections and travel
protocols generated by two weeks of travel
throughout the United States replaces
snapshots of an otherwise ubiquitous
urbanism

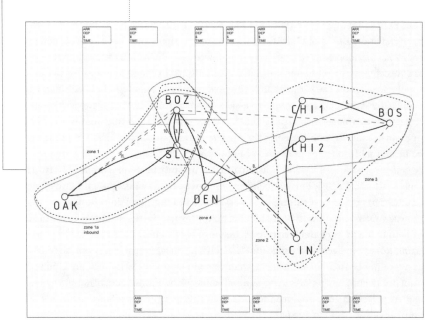

not. For architecture, networks were powerful symbols that served various critical and ideological functions over the last one hundred years, first of a technically liberated and connected globe in the 1930s, and later transforming into a symbol of social democracy built on bodies and machines in the 1960s and 1970s. The connotations of the network image changed after World War II from that of a technical infrastructure to an association with resistance, subversion, and anti-hierarchy, which in turn came to be associated more strongly with the principles of social techno-democracy which inspired architectural practices such as Archigram, Superstudio, Team 10, and so on. Their networks were pure propaganda, the image of a futuristic yet probable technology granting authenticity to an agenda of architectural dissent. Images of networks acted in architecture as the foundation of a plausible aesthetic other, resisting the homogeneity of international modernism and the cronies of the London County Council. Networks provided the technical and social imagery that powered a critical dialogue on the environment and society toward the end of the second era of modernism.[4] Architecture's role was to translate the technical promise of networks into social/spatial terms through exhibitions, drawings, models, and collages. While remaining for the most part technically inspirational fantasies, networks were nonetheless polemically invaluable.[5]

In the last forty-five years, however, the split between the commonly understood image of networks and what they actually signify—that is, the reality of network technologies and organizations—has become a full-blown schizophrenia, one that is at the heart of networks today not only as they are perceived but as they operate. The image of the network symbolizing freedom and democracy through technology has remained essentially stable since the 1960s, while the complexity of the material and abstract organizations of networks as they construct our environment today has developed toward another paradigm entirely. Various strata of networks are revealed within this schism that are usually conflated and speak to a complex topological condition, yet need to be defined and understood as nuanced in and of themselves. Within the scope of this essay I identify three kinds of networks that are linked but distinct—network as symbol, network as infrastructure, and network as organizational diagram or geometry—each of which participate in and are motivated by this schizophrenia in one way or another.

If the image of networks has remained constant, the development of network logic since the 1960s is best characterized as an evolution of geometry. Network geometries have morphed through the classic stages of node and link chain networks, to decentralized and bus type distributions, to the distributed meshes diagrammed by Paul Baran at the Rand Institute at the dawn of the internet.[6] But as each node in Baran's diagram became an endpoint in itself, the two-dimensional geometry of the diagram has been pushed past a state of causal Euclidian clarity into an exponentially more complex topological realm of connection founded on both hierarchical *and* anti-hierarchical structures. Anticipating this development, Marshall McLuhan put it this way: "Euclidian space is the prerogative of visual and literate man. With

This opportunistic summer vacation spot has sprung up along the San Francisco/Los Angeles corridor north of Ventura. Situated on the shoulder of old Highway 1, the location for this ad hoc five-mile-long camper colony is squeezed between the ocean on one side and heavy rail lines and the eight-lane 101 freeway on the other.

Beau Trincia, Ambient Structure, 2006. Study of the development of architectural organizational diagrams.

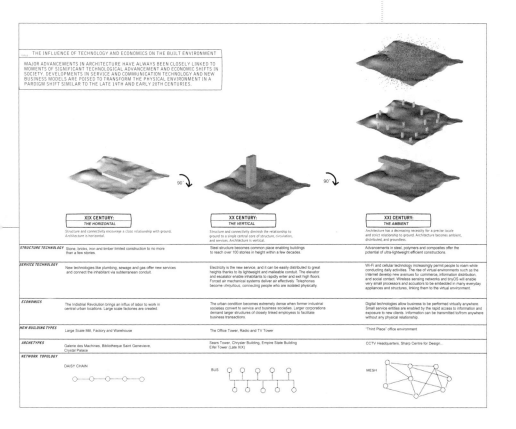

THE INFLUENCE OF TECHNOLOGY AND ECONOMICS ON THE BUILT ENVIRONMENT

MAJOR ADVANCEMENTS IN ARCHITECTURE HAVE ALWAYS BEEN CLOSELY LINKED TO MOMENTS OF SIGNIFICANT TECHNOLOGICAL ADVANCEMENT AND ECONOMIC SHIFTS IN SOCIETY. DEVELOPMENTS IN SERVICE AND COMMUNICATION TECHNOLOGY AND NEW BUSINESS MODELS ARE POISED TO TRANSFORM THE PHYSICAL ENVIRONMENT IN A PARADIGM SHIFT SIMILAR TO THE LATE 19TH AND EARLY 20TH CENTURIES.

	XIX CENTURY: THE HORIZONTAL	XX CENTURY: THE VERTICAL	XXI CENTURY: THE AMBIENT
	Structure and connectivity encourage a close relationship with ground. Architecture is horizontal.	Structure and connectivity diminish the relationship to ground to a single central core of structure, circulation, and services. Architecture is vertical.	Architecture has a decreasing necessity for a precise locale and strict relationship to ground. Architecture becomes ambient, distributed, and groundless.
STRUCTURE TECHNOLOGY	Stone, bricks, iron and timber limited construction to no more than a few stories.	Steel structure becomes common place enabling buildings to reach over 100 stories in height within a few decades.	Advancements in steel, polymers and composites offer the potential of ultra-lightweight efficient constructions.
SERVICE TECHNOLOGY	New technologies like plumbing, sewage and gas offer new services and connect the inhabitant via subterranean conduit.	Electricity is the new service, and it can be easily distributed to great heights thanks to its lightweight and malleable conduit. The elevator and escalator enable inhabitants to rapidly enter and exit high floors. Forced air mechanical systems deliver air effectively. Telephones become ubiquitous, connecting people who are isolated physically.	Wi-Fi and cellular technology increasingly permit people to roam while conducting daily activities. The rise of virtual environments such as the Internet develop new avenues for commerce, information distribution, and social contact. Wireless sensing networks and tinyOS will enable very small processors and accuators to be embedded in many everyday appliances and structures, linking them to the virtual environment.
ECONOMICS	The Industrial Revolution brings an influx of labor to work in central urban locations. Large scale factories are created.	The urban condition becomes extremely dense when former industrial societies convert to service and business societies. Larger corporations demand larger structures of closely linked employees to facilitate business transactions.	Digital technologies allow business to be performed virtually anywhere. Small service entities are enabled by the rapid access to information and exposure to new clients. Information can be transmitted to/from anywhere without any physical relationship.
NEW BUILDING TYPES	Large Scale Mill, Factory and Warehouse	The Office Tower, Radio and TV Tower	'Third Place' office environment
ARCHETYPES	Galerie des Machines, Bibliotheque Saint Genevieve, Crystal Palace	Sears Tower, Chrysler Building, Empire State Building Eifel Tower (Late XIX)	CCTV Headquarters, Sharp Centre for Design...
NETWORK TOPOLOGY	DAISY CHAIN	BUS	MESH

the advent of electric circuitry and the instant movement of information, Euclidean space recedes and the non-Euclidian geometries emerge."[7]

By virtue of their geometric development, networks as abstract organizational diagrams and as material infrastructures have become *the* organizational paradigm. Underscoring the totality of this position, sociologist and urban theorist Manuel Castells writes, "Networks constitute the new social morphology of our societies, and the diffusion of networking logic substantially modifies the operation and outcomes in processes of production, experience, power and culture."[8] Spatially indeterminate, temporally contingent, unstable, inclusive, and dynamic, networks capture the both/and condition of paradoxical inclusion more aligned to quantum mechanics than the either/or of a discursive modernism. Contemporary network formations are founded on the incompatibility and generative tension of two opposing diagrams of organization, or what Alexander Galloway, in his study of network protocols, refers to as the "contradiction between two opposing machines."[9] This condition has been explored in political terms through Michael Hardt and Antonio Negri's book *Empire*, in sociological terms in Castells's *Network Society*, and in digital/material terms as Galloway and Eugene Thacker begin to address in *Protocol*.[10]

Infrastructural and organizational networks today are complex, yet tend toward a natural state of *invisibility*. From communications networks to the organizational abstractions of "netcentric warfare,"[11] the complexity of today's network organizations exceed visualization. As new-media theorists Geert Lovink and Florian Schneider point out, "The networking paradigm escapes the centrality of the icon to visual culture and its critics and instead focuses on more abstract, invisible, subtle processes and feedback loops. There is nothing spectacular about networking."[12] How the networked society can be represented is a question that echoes Fredric Jameson's call fifteen years ago for the production of new visual vocabularies to combat "the incapacity of our minds, at least at present, to map the great global multinational and decentered communicational network in which we find ourselves caught as individual subjects."[13]

Yet despite their invisibility, or precisely because of it, networks are the organizational abstraction *du jour*. Their role in the popular imagination remains a cliché of technologically founded liberation through the tropes of connection, anti-hierarchy, access, and "freedom" applicable to new modes of socialization such as MySpace. The connotations of freedom, democracy, and egalitarianism are used to sell both White House policy at one end of the spectrum and the commercial dream of the first "must have" personalized infrastructure (the net, cell phones, BlackBerrys, etc.) to the gadget-crazed consumer desires of the middle class at the other. As Verizon Wireless advertises simply, "It's *the* network."

The organizational diagram of networks has evolved to encompass a much larger ideological constituency and is applied to everything from the war on terror and domestic surveillance to the pro-technology neo-Marxist discussions of resistance to Empire.[14] While networks as infrastructures, technologies, and organizational abstractions have geometrically and technically evolved, in the popular imagination their signification has largely stood still. The technical liberatory image of networks has been decoupled from the reality of its opposite—that is, networks as a form of distributed and ubiquitous control. It is important then to distinguish the image of networks from the networks themselves for, as Thacker points out, "in the discourses surrounding networks, the tropes of connectivity, collectivity, and participation obscure the material practices of networks."[15] The reality of their technical and organizational complexity and their geometric transition shifts the complicated balance between the semantic and material understanding of networks. The image of the network has been repurposed from a tool of emancipation to a mask for the more complex flows of their material application that have remained until recently beyond critique. And as the conventions of resistance have been co-opted, it is as though meaningful discussion of networks ended with the evolution of iTunes. Thankfully this is changing as a post-digital space of theory and practice led by groups such as the Critical Art Ensemble are now emerging from the backchannels of the internet through new forms of discourse such as blogs, wikis, and chats.

It is important also to keep in mind that unlike the hypnotic power that technology wielded even ten years ago, information technology has matured to the point where access to communication and information networks is pedestrian—an expectation although perhaps not a right. Now more than two generations implicitly understand networks not as an image or an idea but through practice. As McLuhan suggests, "In the age of information, it is information itself that becomes environmental."[16] The activated electromagnetic spectrum that is so fundamental to contemporary devices and technologies known as the Hertzian landscape[17] is testimony to McLuhan's point and has become a regularly traversed territory and a diffuse new layer of urban context usually ignored by architects and urban planners.

The understanding of technology as a pervasive infrastructure or environment forms the core of the ubiquitous computing movement, begun in the late 1980s by Mark Weiser at Xerox Parc.[18] Summarizing the goals of ubiquitous computing, Weiser writes, "The most profound technologies are those that disappear. They weave themselves into the fabric of everyday life until they are indistinguishable from it."[19] The aim of ubiquitous computing is to recenter the human being again in the relationship between humans and technology by embedding computers into our surroundings. Now that the celebration of networks for their technical capabilities that sponsored the dot-com era has subsided, the focus has broadened to include concerns for their implications in non-technical and non-commercial terms. This is especially present in the arts, such as the emerging field of locative media (see below) and the more established net art movement, for example. However, a critical mass has formed around a more developed discussion of networks that includes architecture, as art practice, design, and research are coupled with the emergence of a pro-technology post-internet stance in critical theory through organizations or websites like Rhizome, Nettime, the V2 Organization, and NEURO.[20]

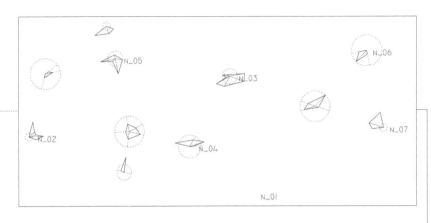

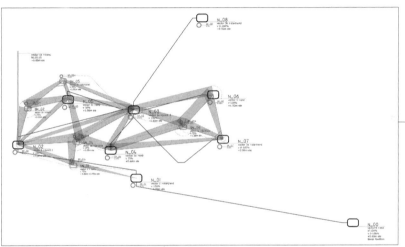

Anthony Burke, Summer Pavilion, 2006,
schematic design. An organizational
network was used as a starting point for
this project, building into a complex
design space through the integration
of specific data sets concerning shade
gradients, user flow and speed, and
hydrology parameters. This diagram shows
location of shade points with initial
shading coefficients and link orientation.

Shade gradients and node/subnode
parameters

Program variables and thresholds

Contingent zones of activities

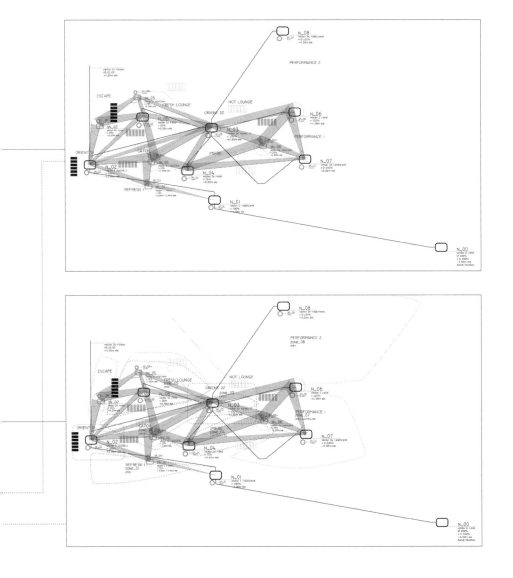

So there is no novelty to the discussion of networks, particularly in their relation to architecture and design, whose histories are tightly intertwined. Indeed, they have been discussed more or less as an inevitable outgrowth of electronic technologies since the beginning of the twentieth century. Yet it is clear we are no longer discussing the same thing. Networks have developed a split personality, and the entrenchment of networks as the dominant hegemony of control and their morph into a pliable topological state that resists dialectics demand a renewed enthusiasm for interrogation in the post-complexity era. Across all disciplines, questions concerning autonomy, subjectivity, control, resistance, surveillance, privacy, agency, visualization, collectivity, and intelligence are once again being addressed, as well as the perennial question, what is to be done?

These new questions are no less important to architecture as entirely new environmental (Hertzian), contextual, and social registers have emerged as a result of network technologies and topologies that challenge our understanding of place and process. Similarly, novel forms of practice are being explored that capitalize on new network models and allow for a highly distributed and agile global presence even for small practices.[21] However, tied intimately to its tools of visualization, architecture has always worked with representations of abstractions, and the development of architecture depends on its ability to address Jameson's concerns for the invention of new visual vocabularies capable of dealing with real complexity. Architecture's role in translating the technical into the social is in desperate need of renewal within this netcentric framework. As the discussions around technology and networks move into a more mature phase of human-centered design, perhaps the most pressing question for architecture to address is how to again locate the "subject" in today's environment.

Manuel Castells has articulated this as a concern for the "structural schizophrenia between function and meaning," from which "there follows a fundamental split between abstract, universal instrumentalism, and historically rooted, particularistic identities. Our societies are increasingly structured around a bipolar opposition between the net and the self."[22] Who are we designing for? What are their needs? What are their practices and how do they construct their own environments through new technologies at their disposal?

Within this split condition between the semantic stasis of networks and new, highly complex network technologies and organizations, lurks the real fear of the impotence of architecture to address the contemporary environment, just as theory itself is being questioned in the age of real-time events.[23] As Gropius reminds us, however, change is fundamental to architecture. As the nature of design is requalified in netcentric terms, architecture has begun to respond. What is emerging is an organizational architecture based on negotiation and contractual formation capable of activating the potential of networked material, technical, and environmental intelligence. Through the design of organizational schema and the control of information exchange, architecture is beginning to address the creative potential of network praxis through what might be thought of as a *protocological architecture*.

Network of One:[24] The Work of Mark Lombardi

The fourth version of Mark Lombardi's monumental 52 by 138–inch drawing *BCCI-ICIC & FAB, 1972–91*, shown at the P.S.1 exhibition Greater New York in 2000, is a highly self-conscious aesthetic expression of a "1960s New Left Liberal in a late-twentieth-century New Right World."[25] The drawing illustrates a network of relationships developed over nineteen years of "black" banking practices that took place behind the stable and profitable facade of the Bank of Credit and Commerce International (BCCI) and the International Credit and Investment Corporation (ICIC), between 1972 and 1991. The drawing links the intelligence agencies of the United States, the United Kingdom, Pakistan, the United Arab Emirates, and Saudi Arabia through the BCCI & ICIC to "a panoply of international gangsters, arms dealers, bagmen, corrupt foreign officials, drug smugglers, tax evaders, money launderers, and agents of influence."[26] As Lombardi's last large drawing before his death, it epitomized the *Narrative Structures* series that he had been developing since 1994.[27]

Lombardi's networks ranged from the connection of American presidents and the arming of Saddam Hussein in the Iran-Iraq war between 1980–88 to the flow of funds through the Vatican's private bank involving characters such as Mussolini, the IRA, and other terrorist groups.[28] His work comes from obsessive research into facts mined from other networks of public information, such as newspapers, magazines, and the internet, which were transferred into card files so extensive (over 14,000 in 2000) they were, in the case of the *BCCI-ICIC*, of interest to the FBI after 9/11. Yet among the objectivity of his fact finding and excruciating research, what Lombardi's work emphasizes is precisely the *opposite* of that assumed horizontal continuum of popularly imagined networks; that is, a point of concentration for the creative potential of a politically motivated *subjective* expression.

Through the development of his *Narrative Structures*, Lombardi combined corporatized models for the envisioning of information[29] with an aesthetic critique of Marx derived from Herbert Marcuse, and it is through this internal dynamic that he was able to create a platform for his resistance to the developing new world order of the late 1980s now more generally recognized as globalization. Lombardi considered his own work very self-consciously as a counterpoint to the dominant hegemony of the developing control society, precisely through choosing to work within the visual information practices that it employs. Lombardi saw networks as both the prevailing diagram of power as well as simultaneously a means toward its resistance.

Lombardi examines a potential outside to the hidden network organizations that engulf us today. As if standing among the trees, where all we can see are connections, Lombardi offers us a view of the forest. His drawings are intentionally rational, assembling the facts of his research into meaningful yet aesthetized compositions. To Lombardi, networks have strata that can be articulated through highly rationalized form, giving the works authority through the primary geometry of circles, rectangles,

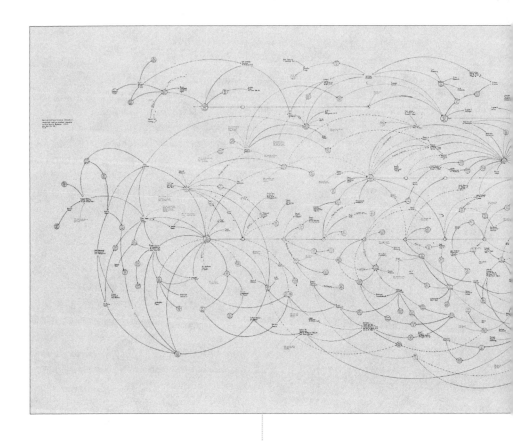

Mark Lombardi, *BCCI-ICIC & FAB, 1972-91*
(4th version, 1996-2000).
Image courtesy of Pierogi and Donald Lombardi.
Whitney Museum of American Art, New York. Purchased
with funds from the Drawing Committee and the
Contemporary Committee

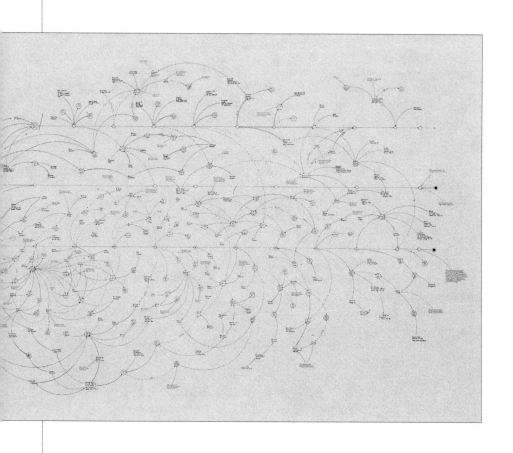

and timelines. Yet he saw his drawings as always in motion, bodies unfinished. His drawings gain a paranoid tension from the interplay between the closed and open systems of form and content, between truth and speculation in a synchronous choreography of facts and relationships. Lombardi sought to make each narrative structure complete within itself, yet "was diametrically opposed to closure."[30]

His drawings, big enough to engulf one's peripheral vision even from a safe viewing distance, provoke the tension between an encompassing objectivity of the content and the visceral and formal subjectivity of their presentation and composition. The bodily impression is replaced by an intellectual impression of the cloying omnipotence of the networks as the detail of Lombardi's illustrations becomes apparent. Although "every statement of fact and connection depicted in the work are true,"[31] the compositions Lombardi created are determinedly personal. Renderings of organizations balance between the authority of flawlessly researched facts and a clarity of overall assembly but with a complicating consciousness "of the need to make these webs cohere into greater constellations that would give each drawing an overall compositional unity."[32]

In attempting to come to terms with contemporary network logics, it is precisely this intentional ambiguity or their topological complexity that make Lombardi's works so illuminating. That Lombardi focuses his work on the networks of political and capital flow, that his drawings and notes are created and stored meticulously by hand at a time when digital printing and archiving mechanisms are routine, only continue to reinstate the subjective interpretive aspect of the works, reinforcing his fundamental resistance to the totalizing networks he illustrates and the "objectivity" of the content he captures.

Lombardi's narrative structures manufacture their own space of existence and resistance within the fluctuations and tensions *between* states—objective facts and subjective composition, open and closed, form and field, truth and fiction—and reveal the inherently unstable dynamic of contemporary networks constructed between two incompatible diagrams of control; centralization and distribution. Indeed, the incompatible diagram is central to the mathematics at the core of contemporary network logics that make them so powerful. Mathematicians Duncan Watts and Steven Strogatz, whose research on small world network dynamics in the early 1990s set the stage for the next generation of network thinking, state the most optimized form of organization is neither fully random nor completely ordered, but somewhere in between.[33] As networks have transformed over the last twenty years from the image of resistance to become the dominant form of control, they have necessarily become inclusive of both hierarchy *and* distribution. Brandon Hookway sums up this creative tension as "the drama of unique existence constantly supplanted by the universal equality of things."[34]

Popular imagination of networks comes from the images of hub and spoke airline charts and the seamlessness of the internet. Usually a symbol of connectivity, equality,

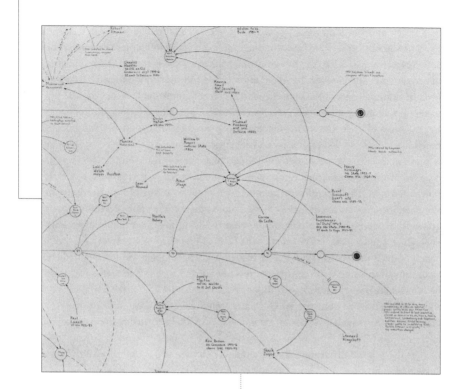

BCCI-ICIC & FAB, 1972-91, detail.

democracy, and freedom, these tropes hide the reality that networks are in fact built upon hegemonic protocols of information exchange required in order to operate. This is Galloway's argument, that the protocols required in the material nature of actual networks, embedded in every packet of information moving around the globe, create a form of absolute control. Networks dependant on the consensual use of standard protocols are temporary, contingent, and fragile in these terms, or as Lovink and Schneider write, "Networked environments are inherently unstable and its temporality is key, much like events. Networks are dense social structures on the brink of collapse and it is questionable if there are sustainable models that can 'freeze' them."[35]

Importantly, Lombardi's work speaks to the potential for creativity and resistance through the dynamics of networks themselves, offering an alternative to twentieth-century forms of protest such as mass demonstrations, strikes, boycotts, and sanctions, which have become ineffectual. In their place other modes of network-enabled resistance have arisen such as the fusing of hacking and activism known as "hacktivism," and the tactical media movement whose goals are to co-opt media against itself through opportunistic projects and interventions.[36] In Lombardi's case, he offers a creative resistance, pushing conventions of network representation past the point of its usual objectivity toward an accelerated and plastic state or hypertrophy that theorists such as Galloway, Lovink, and Pasquinelli have more recently begun to champion.

In the process other questions are raised not only about the possibility of critique and resistance, *but the increasing banality of networking*. As Lovink writes about the absence of a radical critique of network society,

> Instead, we got stuck with remnants of the '68 generation, and the mess they made, characterized by this particular blend of utopia, violence and sell-out. In the past decade collective work on ideas has been replaced by informal networking, a move away from politics toward culture and the arts, shifting the focus toward software, designing interfaces, and just playing around. Instead of blaming the "nettime" generation one could also stress that theory can only grow out of reflected experiences. In that sense we might be too impatient. The question should rather be: how can theory come into being in an age of real-time events?[37]

Rather than being understood as a negative, the structural incompatibility at the heart of network organizations encourages the development of their most notable attributes such as redundancy, contingency, ubiquity, heterogeneity, and flexibility that imbue networks with an unstable yet creative dynamism. In this context, precisely because Lombardi employs the conventions of node and link diagrams, the *Narrative Structures* distinguish themselves through their idiosyncrasies from other forms of network visualization such as the skitter graphs, and plankton maps of CAIDA,[38] questioning the opacity of their authoritative structures. These conventions assign meaning to patterns within information, such as densities, clusters, and gradients, within a completely constructed field, whose forms promote the illusion of naturalized objectivity, continuity, and smoothness that Lombardi resists

Anthony Burke and Eric Paulos, 180x120, 2005. RFID tags track people at the event, projecting their location via a slow-building histogram into the room in real time. The installation is created through mirroring the collective behavior of the crowd, exploring the dynamic between creative collective intelligence and surveillance and control.

Histogram building on local monitor

Tessellated screen embedding predicted behavioral patterns into the depth of the screen's geometry

RFID tags tracked people at the event, logging their behavior through location

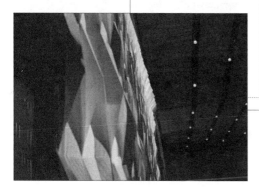

through his compositional drive, recognizing as J. J. King recalls, "Far from being passive object,…maps are instruments of social and political control."[39]

Lombardi seems to play on the topological pliability of networks, and even requires this tension to create the power within his *Narrative Structures*. He articulates the protocols of exchange through a series of symbols for the links devised to articulate the nature of the connections ranging for example from "some type of influence or control" to "sale or transfer of an asset" while the nodes themselves for the most part remain consistent. However, it is the tendency of networks to disappear behind the formal masks of these protocols in favor of a smooth space, to which Lombardi presents an ultimately luddite alternative that avoids technology altogether.

Working in the 1990s, Lombardi's work set a precedent through an analog practice that has, especially since 2000, been taken up vigorously by a growing collection of artists, technologists, programmers, industrial designers, graphic designers, and architects that have begun the task of exploring new visual vocabularies with new technology, seeking also to articulate a new kind of subjectivity within the creative and social potentials of network topologies. Locative media is one of these areas of exploration that encapsulates a very broad range of technologically derived projects, deploying hacked consumer products to highly sophisticated algorithms and specialist equipment. Curator and artist Drew Hemmet defines locative media as that which "uses portable, networked, location aware computing devices for user-led mapping, social networking and artistic interventions in which geographical space becomes its canvas."[40] As a creative practice, locative media ties networks of space, technology, and community together and privileges visualization through collective actions and live experiences to create open projects rather than rarified gallery works.[41]

Time-based city mappings using GPS such as the Amsterdam Realtime 2002 project of the Dutch-based Waag Society articulate personal networks that are overlaid into maps of collective experience and paint a vastly different picture of Amsterdam and its citizens as collaboratory constituents of a dense network space.[42] *PDPal*, a 2003 project by Scott Paterson, Marina Zurkow, and Julian Bleecker overlays user impressions and annotations to a public digital map through hand-held PDAs and a specifically written interface.[43] Both projects build visualizations of networks through interaction, flowing between the agency of the individual and the intelligence of the collective. However, while both build on the conventions of the basemap as a foundation for a network, they are clearly departures from hub-and-spoke formations and privilege new forms of visualization by working with the protocols for assembling and sorting data, without specifying either endpoints or boundaries, only protocols for interaction.[44]

What this type of visualization reveals is not only the creative use of a protocological practice or regime to construct these new visual vocabularies, but a *protocological landscape* itself.[45] By framing new territories through these modes of cartography that privilege open collective structures, the complex protocological landscapes we inhabit are revealed and activated as creative generators by rescripting relationships between actors, technologies, and the environment.

Toward a Protocological Architecture

The architecture we produce will inevitably reveal the degree to which we have been able to show respect for the developing social pattern, which we are part of, without devitalizing our individual contribution to it.
-Walter Gropius[46]

When the high water of continually evolving megastructures paraded in *Archigram* no. 5 and plug-inscapes in *Archigram* no. 6 receded, it revealed a world beyond architecture: a sublime world of pure servicing, information, networking, transience.
-Simon Sadler[47]

Protocols both define environments and offer a potential new suite of creative methods through which architecture may begin to respond to the network dynamics of Hardt and Negri's Empire, "a decentered and deterritorializing apparatus of rule that... manages hybrid identities, flexible hierarchies, and plural exchanges through modulating networks of command."[48] In Galloway's terms, protocol is "a language that regulates flow, directs netspace, codes relationships, and connects life-forms....Protocol is always a second order process; it governs the architecture of the architecture of objects."[49] Protocol is what makes networks and Empire function; they are formal constructs that provide the vitality to network logics, yet they also identify a territory of control points, super-connected hubs of potential leverage within a design context where information is exchanged and regulated. They are trans-scalar or non-scalar in these terms, and in terms of design they may be applied against a material, social, or regional condition with equal effect.

As we operate within the terms of this encompassing material and procedural environment governed by protocol, what we might term a *protocology*, there remains the issue of visualization. Identifying and understanding a landscape in protocological terms is necessary before that knowledge can be turned into an active design agenda. In other words, how might a protocological architecture be activated? Following from Watts and Strogatz, a protocological architecture necessarily exists in the in-between space, the topological fold of both an empowering infrastructural ambience, and points of concentration that effectively organize that ambience. Technically progressive yet without an object-oriented focus, a protocological architecture provides scope for the subject to re-emerge, described and empowered by their constitutive role as design agents. Through negotiating the potentials of material, organizational, and political latency, an *intersubjective* rationalist schema of material and spatial intelligence may be possible. A protocological architecture is an architecture of organization, negotiation, and management whose home is the complexity of the database over the romance of the napkin sketch.

Beau Trincia, Ambient Structure.
Embarcadero Center redevelopment. Diagram
sequence exploring distributed field
potential of program relations based
on program-independent infrastructural
requirements or a program *protocology*.

Advertising field potential

Marketing/public relations field potential

Publishing field potential

Graphic design field potential

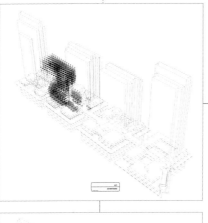

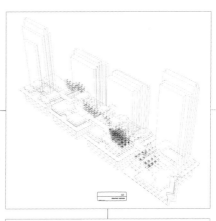

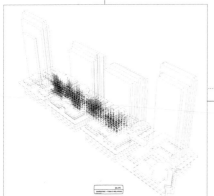

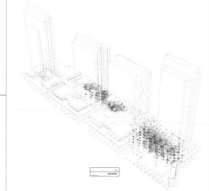

Toward a protocological architecture.
Proposal for structural matrix based
on field potential studies and highest
potential integration of program strata

In architecture we are already witnessing a meta-structural moment, through a renewed appreciation of organizational schema in terms of coding and material patterning as a rich source for design. In this sense a protocological practice is emerging in the hands of a maturing and dexterously digital generation, adept with the abstraction of organization diagrams and network complexity as much as the abstraction of code as a new open source standard of visualization and a living meaningful language. Similarly, as a generation of users executing a mastery over media, engaging with a two-way interactivity completely unlike unidirectional traditional media and architecture is an expectation. In this mediated and interactive environment, assembly and organization create meaning on the fly, forecasting the transformation of the architect necessarily along the lines of the negotiator. Design becomes the ability to schematize organizational structures and activate relationships using unique, purpose-built, and intelligent software tools.[50]

Understanding the vanishing of the object into an empathetic appreciation of field, presence, process, and the immanent establishes a vector of exploration for both the architect as its own subject and ambitions for novel forms of spatial articulation which can accommodate this form of topological complexity, not as a formal metaphor but as an open protocological schema. Recognizing the opportunities within the pliable topology of network geometries, a protocological architecture allows for the realignment of both semantic aspect of networks to their advanced technical and political condition that have become uncoupled in design through its inclusive organizational and pre-formal logic. A protocology of place and practice creates opportunities for architecture to again address broader questions of space and meaning, politics and power that have recently been largely ignored by the vanguard in favor of superficial obsessions, or obsessions *with surface*, centered on the recent yet strangely exhausted technologies of CNC routers and 3D printers.

While networks were a visionary apparatus initially for the technologically impelled megalomania of the likes of Buckminster Fuller and Constantinos Doxiadis,[51] before transforming and humanizing into the radical visions of the 1960s, today they have exchanged their polemical capacity for a ubiquitous materiality and agency. Less talk, more action. As Castells continuously points out, the network paradigm is not only technological but social and economic, and it is now that we need to construct a critical and creative practice that recognizes this condition. In contemporary architectural terms, network practices have been couched in an almost single-minded techno-utopian revival of a happy and inevitable past-future, with a Marimekko-patterned aesthetic to match. However, by attempting to continually synthesize the complexities of the political and material aspects of networks, by embracing this dynamic, architecture is able to construct a new form of generative and creative practice, perhaps even while coming to terms with its new subject. While being overwhelmed by a tsunami of technical affordances, architecture needs once again to critically interpret their human value through the spatial consequences and opportunities of the flows that have been put in motion by the technologies we have so eagerly consumed.

Verizon Wireless billboard advertisement, 2006

Notes

··········

Epigraph: Walter Gropius, *Scope of Total Architecture* (New York: Harper and Row, 1943), 75; Gilles Deleuze and Félix Guattari, *A Thousand Plateaus: Capitalism and Schizophrenia* (Minneapolis: University of Minnesota Press, 1987), 500.

1...Clay Shirky, "Rip the Consumer," http://www.shirky.com/writings/consumer.html (accessed June 20, 2006). Shirky writes, "We have often heard that Internet puts power in the hands of the consumer, but this is nonsense—'powerful consumer' is an oxymoron."

2...Michael Hardt and Antonio Negri, *Empire,* (Cambridge, MA: Harvard University Press, 2000).

3...Alexander Galloway, *Protocol: How Control Exists after Decentralization* (Cambridge, MA: MIT Press, 2004), 147.

4...For more detailed discussions, see Mark Wigley, "Network Fever" in *Grey Room* 4 (Summer 2001); and Simon Sadler, *Archigram: Architecture without Architecture* (Cambridge, MA: MIT Press, 2005).

5...This is not to ignore the fact that Archigram and other radical practices of the 1960s and '70s era did build and did position their practices and work in some instances as very real proposals for real spaces. However, the majority of their work, and their self-confessed interest in media and employing new tools of architectural production such as the 'zine *Archigram*, makes their work important for the discourse it generated, the new tools of production they championed, the utopias they imagined, and the establishment they sought to undermine.

6...Paul Baran's paper, "On Distributed Communications: 1 Introduction to Distributed Communications Networks" (Rand Corporation Memorandum, RM-3420-PR, Aug. 1964) is generally recognized as the research model that gave rise to the network logics that underpin the internet as we know it today.

7...Marshall McLuhan, "The Relation of the Environment to the Anti-environment," in *Marshall McLuhan—Unbound*, 4th ed. (Corte Madera, CA: Ginko Press, 2005), 15.

8...Manuel Castells, *The Information Age: Economy, Society and Culture; Volume 1: The Rise of the Network Society*, 2nd ed. (Malden, MA: Blackwell, 2000), 500.

9...Galloway, *Protocol*, 8.

10...Hardt and Negri, *Empire*; Castells, *The Information Age*; Galloway, *Protocol*.

11...Netcentric warfare is an initiative launched by the U.S. Secretary of Defense Donald Rumsfeld in 2003. This topic was perhaps first studied by John Arquilla and David Rosenfeldt in publications such as "The Advent of Netwar," (Rand Monograph report, Rand Institute, 1996), and "Networks and Netwars: The Future of Terror Crime and Militancy (Rand, 2001).

12...Geert Lovink and Florian Schneider, "Notes on the State of Networking," Makeworlds-Paper no. 4, Submitted by fls on Sun, 04/04/2004—16:51. http://makeworlds.org/node/100 (accessed May 26, 2006).

13...Frederic Jameson, "The Cultural Logic of Late Capitalism," in *Postmodernism, or The Cultural Logic of Late Capitalism* (Durham: Duke University Press, 1991), 44, and quoted in Brian Holms, "Counter Cartographies," in Janet Abrams and Peter Hall, eds., *Else/Where: Mapping, New Cartographies of Networks and Territories* (Minneapolis: University of Minnesota Press, 2006), 20.

14...As a recent example of the complex topology of the conflated infrastructural political and media networks, in the first days of the Israeli campaign against Hezbollah in July 2006, text messages were being sent by unknown sources into Lebanon warning of impending bombings that never happened. Whether this was a propaganda campaign or a real warning and from which faction in the conflict was not clear, yet the response from citizens was immediate and proliferated widely.

15...Eugene Thacker, "Protocol is as Protocol Does," foreword to Galloway, *Protocol*, xviii.

16...McLuhan, "The Relation of the Environment to the Anti-environment," 17.

17...Hertzian space: A term derived from the name of German Physicist Heinrich Rudolf Hertz (1857–1894), who was the first to produce electromagnetic waves artificially. The concept of Hertzian space was popularized by Anthony Dunne in his book *Hertzian Tales: Electronic Products, Aesthetic Experience and Critical Design* (London: Royal College of Art, 1994) and later expanded on in Anthony Dunne and Fiona Raby, "Tunable Cities," *Architectural Design* (Nov.–Dec. 1998), as well as in their book *Design Noir: The Secret Life of Electronic Objects* (Basel: Birkhauser, 2001). Thanks to Alison Sant for this background.

18…Mark Weiser, considered to be the father of ubiquitous computing. For more see http://www.ubiq.com/weiser/ (accessed Aug. 21, 2006).

19…Mark Weiser, "The Computer for the Twenty-First Century," *Scientific American,* (September 1991): 94–100; http://www.ubiq.com/hypertext/weiser/SciAmDraft3.html (accessed Aug. 21, 2006).

20…In fact these websites and organizations have been operating in parallel with the development of the internet, and now matured into hubs for critical reflection on new media, networks, and other internet-related issues. See http://www.rhizome.org; http://www.nettime.org; http://www.v2.nl; and http://www.neuro.kein.org.

21…See Christopher Hight, "Scalar Networks, Super Creeps: Approaching the Non-Standard in the Architecture of Servo," in this volume.

22…Castells, *The Information Age*, 3.

23…Lovink and Schneider, "Notes on the State of Networking."

24…I first used this phrase in my own practice around 2003, but was reminded of it recently in an article on Mark Lombardi by Frances Richard published for the online magazine Wburg.com in the winter of 2002 and in part in Robert Hobbs, *Mark Lombardi Global Networks* (New York: Independent Curators International, 2004) the catalog that accompanied a 2003 traveling exhibition. The quote reads, "In combination, the two terms epitomize the figure of the artist as compulsive articulator, a solitary node tying collective experience together." Frances Richard, "Toward a Diagram of Mark Lombardi," http://wburg.com/0202/arts/pdfs/lombardi.pdf (page 7) (accessed June 12, 2006).

25…Hobbs, *Mark Lombardi Global Networks*, 49.

26…Ibid., 96.

27…Ibid., 13.

28…See Lombardi's pieces *Banco Nazionale del Lavoro, Reagan, Bush, & Thatcher and the Arming of Iraq, ca 1979–90* (4th version) and *Inner Sanctum: The Pope and His Bankers Michele Sindona and Roberto Calvi, ca. 1959–82* (5th version) in Hobbs, *Mark Lombardi Global Networks*, 88–89 and 62–63, respectively.

29…Edward R. Tufte's book, *Envisioning Information* (Cheshire, CT: Graphics Press, 1990), among other sources, provided a foundation for the development of Lombardi's *Narrative Structures.*

30…Hobbs, *Mark Lombardi Global Networks,* 14.

31…Ibid., 52.

32…Ibid.

33…Duncan Watts and Steven Strogatz, "Collective Dynamics of Small World Networks" *Nature* 393 (June 4, 1998): 440–42.

34…Brandon Hookway, *Pandemonium: The Rise of Predatory Locales in the Postwar World* (New York: Princeton Architectural Press, 1999), 81.

35…Lovink and Schneider, "Notes on the State of Networking."

36…For various definitions of tactical media, see www.nyu.edu/fas/projects/vcb/definingTM.html (accessed Aug. 21, 2006).

37…Lovink and Schneider, "Notes on the State of Networking."

38…CAIDA (The Cooperative Association for Internet Data Analysis), at the University of California, San Diego; see http://www.caida.org/home/ (accessed Aug. 21, 2006).

39…J. J. King, "The Node Knows," in Abrams and Hall, eds. *Else/Where*, 44.

40…Drew Hemmet "Locative Dystopia" (2004), http://www.drewhemment.com/2004/locative_dystopia_2.html (accessed July 2006); reference courtesy of Alison Sant.

41…For more on locative media, see http://www.locative.net (accessed Aug. 21, 2006).

42…http://www.waag.org/project/amsterdamrealtime (accessed Aug. 21, 2006).

43…http://www.pdpal.com/ (accessed Aug. 21, 2006).

44…See also Alison Sant, *Redefining the Basemap*, http://www.alisant.net/published.html (accessed Aug. 21, 2006). Sant would argue that by relying on the basemap that they reinforce our notions of spatial hierarchy which could be transformed by thinking about networks as another spatial organization.

45…Keller Easterling has conducted significant research into this kind of ecology since the mid 1990s. See Keller Easterling, *Organizational Space: Landscapes, Highways and Houses in America* (Cambridge, MA: MIT Press, 2001).

46…Gropius, *Scope of Total Architecture*, xxi.

47…Sadler, *Archigram*, 93.

48…Hardt and Negri, *Empire*, xii.

49…Galloway, *Protocol*, 75.

50…For further exploration of this point, see Anthony Burke, "After BitTorrent; Darknet to Native Data," in Chris Hight and Chris Perry, eds., "Collective Intelligence," special issue, *AD* (2007).

51…See Wigley, "Network Fever," for more on the relationship between Doxiadis, Fuller, and McLuhan.

Biological Networks: On Neurons, Cellular Automata, and Relational Architectures

Therese Tierney

Can complexity be built on simplicity? Or more specifically, can simple computational programs model complex natural systems? Today, the answer may seem deceptively clear, but the path researchers took in attempting to answer this question was neither easy nor straightforward. By retracing the twentieth-century advancement of mathematics, computer science, and neurology, one finds evidence of a sustained inquiry into the principles and dynamics of structure and interaction. During the 1940s, this inquiry required a philosophical shift away from singular models of design toward a dynamic interconnected systems approach. Numerous iterations and reinterpretations formed a complex feedback loop between solitary research and interdisciplinary collaborations, hinging on how the discrete sciences conceptualized physical phenomena related to time, growth, and development. Within each of these disciplines, researchers were finally pressed to acknowledge the limitations of previous paradigms. These paradigms in turn gave way to the development of new informatic models, which recognized the importance of relational dynamics within network morphologies.

What is commonly shared by mathematics, computation, and neurology is the study of organization, its structure and function. What is less evident is that their evolution entailed collaborative work on nonlinear developmental models. One of the early moves in this direction occurred when the philosopher/mathematician Alfred North Whitehead proposed that process rather than substance was the fundamental constituent of the world and that nature consisted of patterns of activity.[1] His theoretical investigations led him to conclude that process produces, elaborates, and maintains the form or structure of material and organisms and that it consists

Evidence of computation in biological forms. Most of these formal systems are simple enough that they can be generated by simple programs. Many exhibit either geometrical shapes or repetition of identical elements. A few, however, employ various types of nesting.

Leaf systems. The full array of patterns that can be produced by simple substitution systems in which each stem branches into exactly two symmetrical stems at each step.

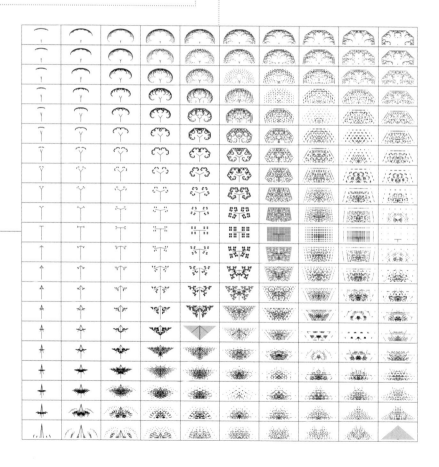

of a complex series of exchanges between an organism and its environment. Form and behavior emerges from process. Thus process has priority over product—both ontologically and epistemologically.[2]

While the implications of this line of reasoning can be extended to design research, the processist view suggests that understanding form is not as important as understanding the processes in which form is embedded. Form and behavior emerge from processes of complex systems.

If we broaden Whitehead's theories to include a computational approach, algorithms can be construed as processes. Scripting employs inductive strategies to model generative processes or simulate complex phenomena.[3] As processes, algorithmic models inhabit space, time, and type. To be more specific, algorithms have a certain temporal and structural coherence, which is formally constructed and intrinsic to its operations. Thus when a program is run, a process is instantiated. Furthermore the algorithm, or subprogram, is developmental in that it can be structured in a recursive or iterative way, so that it modifies or develops over time. For processists, change of every sort—physical, organic, psychological—is a pervasive and predominant feature. For process philosophy, what a thing *is*, as with an algorithmic model, consists in what it *does*.

In this sense, computational biology can describe structure and organization as relationships of interdependence and connection with respect to design investigations. A relational model is significant because the production of form in biological systems exhibits an irreducible complexity, as well as a non-linear method of organization related to networks and distributed models. While complex formal geometries must have a thorough grounding in mathematics, it is also possible to conceptualize processes and systems as a result of simple computational strategies, which then produce complexity. This method affords a new mode of analysis, one in which structured behavior emerges from the interaction of simple rules. Rather than merely serving as an analogy, computational models can be used to generate and test designs, as well as to evolve forms and structures, allowing us to think about design in new ways.

The Manhattan Project

> We used to believe that if we knew one thing and then another, then we know two, because one and one are two. We are now discovering that we must learn more about the "and."
> —Arthur Eddington[4]

Less than eight decades ago, the modern discipline of computer science was nonexistent. Physics and mathematics were separate and discrete disciplines: physics concentrated on forces related to physical phenomena while mathematics explored abstract rules. Any experimental research related to computation would therefore have to cross disciplinary boundaries.

During the late 1940s, the mathematician John von Neumann—who is credited with creating the architecture of the modern computer—was the first to explore the theoretical aspects of cellular automata. His findings were indirectly linked to a search for understanding biological processes—in particular, reproduction. Later he collaborated with the Polish mathematician Stanislaw Ulam, who further refined his ideas. Their work contributed to cellular automata's current formal description and computational application.

From the beginning, von Neumann described computation as *idealized neurons,* rather than electrical-mechanical circuits and vacuum tubes.[5] He did this to separate the logical design from the engineered components, which are used to implement the logical structure. His greatest theoretical contributions were actually in the foundations of quantum mechanics—in set theory, logics, and probabilities—in addition to economics, game theory, and the notion of mechanical reproduction.

Between 1948 and 1949, von Neumann presented a paper called "The General and Logical Theory of Automata." The question he was preoccupied with focused on whether or not it was possible for a machine, or "automaton" as he called it, to reproduce itself.[6] As a technical challenge, it is clearly possible to imagine a machine that could fabricate something much simpler than itself—industrial factories are based on this technology. But could a machine possibly give birth to other machines as complicated as itself? Or is there some extra mechanical "vitalist" notion to self-reproduction? In order to rationalize the problem, von Neumann suggested conceptualizing the theoretical robot or automata as composed of a small number of standardized components:

I will introduce as elementary units neurons, a "muscle," entities which make and cut fixed contacts, and entities which supply energy, all defined with about that degree of superficiality with which [the theory of neural networks] describes an actual neuron. If you describe muscles, connective tissues, "disconnecting tissues," and means of providing metabolic energy...you probably wind up with something like 10 or 12 or 15 elementary parts.[7]

What is particularly fascinating about von Neumann's abstract theory of mechanical reproduction is that his descriptive vocabulary was appropriated from the biological sciences: tissues, muscles, neurons, and growth. His novel concept of reproductive machines consisting of multiple copies of a smaller number of standardized elements raises a question about machinic self-generation:

Can one build an aggregate out of such elements in such a manner that if it is put into a reservoir, in which there float all these elements in large numbers, it will then begin to construct other aggregates, each of which will at the end turn out to be another automaton exactly like the original one?[8]

By applying mathematical logic, von Neumann was then able to conclude that such self-reproduction should in fact be realizable. His proof was conditional on the notion that an automaton could have a set of instructions or an algorithmic program for building itself, and that in self-generation, two steps would be required:

first, make an exact replica of the program; and second, use the program as a set of instructions for making a replica of the robot.[9]

Remarkably, von Neumann seemed to be addressing two separate topics through the application of a scale-free theory. First, he raised the meta-question, how did life originate on Earth? And then the micro-question, how is form generated?[10] While his theories preceded the discovery of the DNA molecule by several years, the role of the computational program could be comparable to the way DNA is used in biological self-reproduction, for here the DNA is both copied and used as instructions for building new proteins.[11]

However, von Neumann's mathematical model and his corresponding formal description of a reservoir full of floating machine parts was unconvincing to other mathematicians at the time. This was due to several reasons. First, the existing mathematical approaches of the time were linear, reductive, and predictive.[12] Second, mathematical calculations were still being computed with analog methods.[13] Overall, it simply fell between disciplines and paradigms. Cellular automata did not fit into the conventional linear problem-solving models of the time, and as a result no further research efforts were put toward the potential new discoveries that could be gained from cellular automata. It would take extraordinary circumstances to create change, to dissolve the political, intellectual, and disciplinary boundaries, and initiate the conditions necessary for interdisciplinary research.

Although von Neumann could not foresee the potential of cellular automata, he had the insight to realize the important difference with this type of reproductive model. Cellular automata are highly productive as models because they visually describe how an algorithm can be a generative tool.[14] They do not require advanced mathematics, only the logic of computation. Cellular automata also relate to observable nature because they can model complex systems and can assist in understanding the patterned activity of neuronal systems.[15] Furthermore researchers can employ them in simplified simulations, creating useful models for studying unpredictability. Unlike simple combinatorics or components in linear assemblies, cellular automata engage in unpredictable, nonlinear, relational behavior.[16]

While von Neumann was experimenting with floating reservoirs in Southern California, Stanislaw Ulam was studying mathematics in Poland. In 1936, facing an impending German invasion, von Neumann invited Ulam to attend the Institute of Advanced Studies at Princeton University. Princeton at that time had become an intellectual center for displaced European scientists, and Ulam, of Jewish descent, quickly accepted.[17] While there, Ulam noticed that many of the scientists were thinking about issues outside of pure mathematics. Von Neumann, the most influential among them, was absorbed with classical problems in physics: problems related to turbulence in hydrodynamics. Could these two disciplines, physics and mathematics, ever converge? At a traditional university, probably not. But in 1943, Ulam was invited to join what he described as "an unidentified project doing important work; the physics having something to do with the interior of the stars."[18] Ulam traveled to

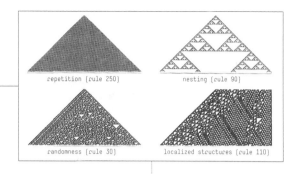

repetition (rule 250)   nesting (rule 90)

randomness (rule 30)   localized structures (rule 110)

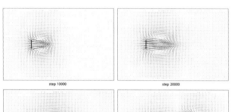

step 10000   step 20000

Four basic examples of behavior produced
by cellular automata with simple
underlying rules. In each case, the
most obvious features vary according to
the rules that were applied. Not all
images shown are at the same scale; the
last image appears coarser because the
structures it contains are larger.

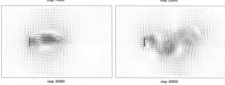

step 30000   step 40000

Particle velocity diagrams. A simple
cellular automaton system is set up
to emulate the behavior of molecules
in a fluid. In each frame there are a
total of 30 million underlying cells.
The individual velocity vectors drawn
correspond to averages over 20x20 blocks
of cells. At each step the configuration
of particles is updated according to
simple collision and reflection rules. The
agreement with experimental results on
actual fluid flows is quite accurate .

step 50000

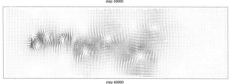

step 60000

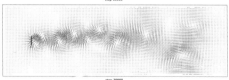

step 70000

Los Alamos where, along with Edward Teller, he subsequently developed the hydrogen bomb.

Ulam's work on the Manhattan Project included statistical neutron multiplication and the calculation of the hydrodynamics problem involved in the implosion process. Around this time, his interests shifted to applied rather than abstract mathematics. In order to develop the bomb, the mathematicians needed advanced computing capabilities unavailable at that time. Ulam, along with Nick Metropolis and von Neumann, invented the Monte Carlo simulation technique, which led to the invention of the modern computer. Through its speed of calculation, the computational engine aided in the solution of numerous computations required to develop the hydrogen bomb.

At the same time, the efforts in computation caused Ulam to rethink some of von Neumann's earlier work on mechanical reproduction. Ulam imagined that cellular automata were structurally linked to developmental growth, to time and change. Ulam's straightforward suggestion was to jettison the "floating machine parts in a reservoir." The automata should instead be conceptualized as an idealized space of cells that could hold finite state-numbers representing different sorts of parts.[19] Ulam's first published reference to this idea reads as follows:

> An interesting field of application for models consisting of an infinite number of interacting elements may exist in the recent theories of automata. A general model, considered by von Neumann and the author, would be of the following sort: Given is an infinite lattice or graph of points, each with a finite number of connections to certain of its "neighbors." Each point is capable of a finite number of "states." The states of neighbors at time tn induce, in a specified manner, the state of the point at time $tn+1$. One aim of the theory is to establish the existence of subsystems which are able to multiply, i.e., create in time other systems identical ("congruent") to themselves.[20]

This follows von Neumann's concept of reproduction but adds the completely new, pivotal idea of a relational or sensitivity-dependent neighbor. The program begins with an initial condition and then the rules modify this condition. With cellular automata, rules are relational—that is to say, they are based on the cell's local relationship to its neighbor. The rules can be quite simple, but over time the cells can change from state to state. When the time comes for the cells to change state, each cell looks around and gathers information on its neighbors' states. (Exactly which cells are considered "neighbors" is also something that depends on the particular cellular automata.) Based on its own state, its neighbors' states, and the rules of the cellular automata, the cell decides what its new state should be. All the cells change state at the same time. The row of cells could be construed as a small "world" that runs through a sequence of "years" or "generations." At the end of each year, all the cells simultaneously decide on their state for the next year. When halted, a completed cellular automata resembles a highly complex pattern comprising of black and white cells, with sub-patterns at different scales. This method of display produces a potentially intricate two-dimensional graphic image, in which one sees the whole evolution of the cellular automata throughout time as a progression.

Organization implies a direction of development; how can structure implicitly describe change? Ulam was consumed with the formal question, where does complexity come from? More importantly, how much information is required for a morphology? The underlying rules in cellular automata can be conceptualized as machine instructions, while the initial conditions can be thought of as rough analogues of the program. The rules are simple, the initial conditions are simple, and yet they result in complex behavior. The formal description merely requires a bottom-up structural logic and then applies simple rules recursively. With this method of organization, a non-periodic structure could exhibit unpredictability, despite the relative simplicity of its recursive relations.[21] Therefore it would be possible to extrapolate that if simple abstract rules are applied mechanistically, they could reproduce the behavior of natural systems.

Yet it must be stressed that as an argument against universality, it is extremely important to note that in contrast to cellular automata, neighbor *independent* substitution systems will only generate patterns that are either repetitive or nested, but only *sequential relational substitution systems* will produce varied complex patterns.

Furthermore, scientists also observed that systems in nature tended toward efficiency or are optimized. In other words, nature uses the most economical method. Cellular automata model a system that autonomously works out an algorithm, or set of rules with resultant unpredictable diversity. The notion that very simple rules could govern complex behavior might begin to explain form-generation, as well as suggest that every process might not need it own explicit rules, but could self-organize. By 1952, Ulam's important suggestion led von Neumann to complete a formal description of a self-reproducing "cellular automaton" that uses twenty-nine states. In retrospect, we can say that Ulam should be credited with the concept of the cells, while von Neumann with that of the automata.[22]

Von Nuemann concluded, "The theory of automata is a subject lying between logics, communication theory and physiology."[23] In retrospect, although von Neumann deployed numerous types of cellular automata, the results were never published in his lifetime nor were they ever simulated due to a lack of computational power. Moreover, a more important failure in von Neumann's reasoning was that he could not imagine the concept of feedback; his theories only encompassed feedforward processes.[24] In contrast, Norbert Weiner was concurrently developing a theory of cybernetics at the Massachusetts Institute of Technology. He described feedback as "a process whereby some proportion or in general, function, of the output signal of a system is passed (fed back) to the input. Often this is done intentionally, in order to control the dynamic behavior of the system."[25]

Unlike Weiner, however, von Neumann also believed that the human mind was logically organized. Although he was the first to conceptualize computational processes as "idealized neurons," von Neumann found it impossible to understand how a biological neural system could have unreliable circuitry and yet still come up with reliable solutions.[26] Trained as a mathematician, his approach was too linear, too sequential to conceptualize neural nets.

Considering the unswerving directionality of Information Engineering Operations Research (IEOR) during the 1940s, von Neumann's rational approach was necessarily focused toward military logistics. Cellular automata's very organizational properties (i.e., relational and unpredictable) went against the then-current scientific belief that the whole could be understood through the sum of its parts and causal methods were employed for statistical predictability.[27] By incorporating feedback, cellular automata exceeded their application beyond linear predictability. Ulam's highly original research contributions generated a simple system of reproduction, based on sensitivity to initial conditions, developed through relational behavior, linked to growth, and undergoing unpredictable change in time and space, which resulted in considerably more than the sum of its parts.[28] Moreover, it was only much later, in 1995, that John Holland's research at the Santa Fe Institute in complexity studies demonstrated that a cellular automata model could be used as a discrete space for the simulation of varying flexible processes: excitable media, biological and chemical morphogenesis, turbulence, biological networks, and tectonic processes.[29] Holland called cellular automata "iterative circuit computers" and proposed that they could be useful in the development of a theory of complex adaptive systems. Though unknown at the time, the principles of a cellular automaton model were harbingers of what subsequently developed into network theory.

Without clearly knowing the implications of cellular automata research, electrical engineers revived many of these same issues after the war during the 1950s. As an outgrowth of IEOR, newly trained systems analysts applied their expertise in computation as a means to visualize the organization of the brain as an "information processor." Already the systems analysts were cognizant that von Neumann's architecture had its limitations. The method was linear, inflexible, and it slowed processing down. Scientists knew that neural networks had a very different kind of architecture. The brain's neural networks consisted of large numbers of much simpler processors, very highly connected with no separate memory. Even with neural networks, however, the question remained: through what models could such a distributed system be conceptualized?

Network structures. These networks represent possible sequences of black and white cells that can occur at successive steps in the evolution of typical class 3 and class 4 cellular automata. The number of nodes in these networks seem to increase at an exponential rate.

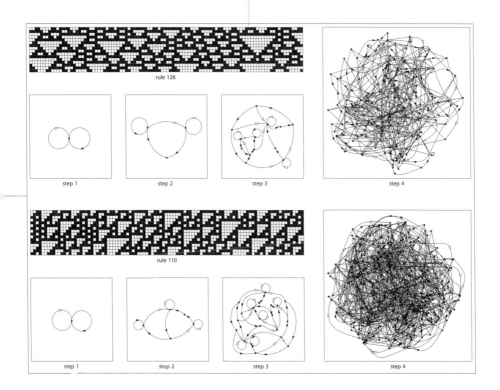

rule 126

step 1   step 2   step 3   step 4

rule 110

step 1   step 2   step 3   step 4

....

> Present day physics represents a limiting case—valid for inanimate objects. It will
> have to be replaced by new laws, based on new concepts, if organisms with con-
> sciousness are to be described.
>
> —Eugene Wigner[30]

How does the brain figure into the development of the computer? Freud might describe
it as an obsessive tendency toward neuronal envy. Consider the situation as it was
presented to computer programmers in the 1970s and early '80s: research had determined that the human genome was simply not large enough to preprogram all possible scenarios that human beings need to function properly in the environment.
And even if the genome could specify this amount of information, the cortex still
lacks adequate surface area to contain it. The fundamental issues at stake here are
the same ones already familiar to information processing—that is to say, information storage, transmission, and compression were completely inexplicable in the human brain. Furthermore, no one knew what mechanisms were at work that allowed
a human organism to generate meaningful information from a dynamic stream of
environmental data.[31]

In 1982, Andrew Coward, a Canadian systems programmer, decided to shift his
research direction. His earlier work in network design led him to the realization
that there were limitations in the von Neumann architecture. Reactions to his paper, "A Connectionist Alternative to the von Neumann Architecture," made him realize that he was not alone in this line of thinking.[32] As a calculator and data processor, the conventional computer was adequate. There was the centralized processing
unit separate from memory storage which stores data before and after processing
and holds immediate results. Because each operating element was isolated, information was continually pushed back and forth between the processor and memory. It
solved problems linearly, sequentially, rigidly—that is to say, one at a time. The brain
would never be able to respond to environmental demands if it solved problems in
the same manner. Yet the brain was a fraction of the size of a super computer. While
Coward knew that the answer lay in parallel distributed processing, he was more
interested in understanding the coarse-grained relations within the human neuronal system.[33] Motivated by an organizational curiosity at the system level, Coward
wanted to know how to design complexity without being complex. By rejecting the
then-prevalent theory, "sensory input to action,"[34] he began by applying network
theories and network system design to the brain.

Is it possible to understand the brain as a system? To get to the bottom of
Coward's research, it will be necessary to look at what the neurons are actually doing at the molecular level. The first problem encountered is that there is not only
one standard model of a neuron. Simultaneously, each individual neuron cell can

change form. The entire neural network is vastly flexible and kinetic, with infinite connective possibilities between neurons. As the biophysicist Floyd Ratliff points out, there are in fact "great variations in cell type, synaptic type, transmitter, pre-, epi- and post-synaptic mechanisms, graded transmitter release, regional specialization within the neuron, and other similar factors."[35] Neurons then can have very different physical appearances and respond in different ways to electrical and chemical factors, neurotransmitters and neurohormones, which alter according to the contextual environment of the axons. On a global scale, different regions in the brain also exhibit very different morphology and connectivity. Is there some unifying concept or model that explains this diversity of form and operation?

Most of the higher mental functions, that is to say the thinking, occur in the neocortex. The neocortex contains some 100 billion cells, each with 1,000 to 10,000 connective synapses and has approximately 900 million linear feet of wiring.[36] Viewed systematically, the neuron is an information-processing unit that transforms many input signals into a single output channel. A typical neuron receives 1,000 to 10,000 incoming axonometric signals; inputs come from many other axons of other neighboring neurons. As incoming information, the signal's presence or absence, like a 0 or a 1, has an effect, like dots and dashes of a Morse code.

To understand the operative principles of the brain, we have to extract a set of concepts that are meaningful on both the system level and sufficiently general to adequately represent the wide range of variation at the detailed operational level. Is there a concept that can be meaningful on both levels? With programming, Coward knew the two important concepts were instructions and data.[37] The functioning of a computer system is then understood as the execution of a sequence of instructions acting on a body of data. Without being reductive, is it still possible to create a model of neuronal activity?

Coward proposed that the brain can be understood as a modulated pattern extraction hierarchy. Note that this hierarchy is a network of pattern-recognition units in which a selection of input signals determines if a high enough proportion of its programmed pattern is present, in which case the identified pattern also signals (output). The inputs come from other units and represent the presence or absence of other, usually simpler patterns. Therefore, the brain can be conceptualized as a pattern extraction template, in which successive layers are able to extract more and more complex patterns from relatively simple input. The template forms a hierarchy in connectivity space even though some layers may vary in location.[38]

As if that wasn't complex enough, sensory input sets up a combination of neuron firings, which are then available wherever those axons are connected in the brain. The proportion of signal input at which a unit will fire is determined by its arousal level, which is determined by the strength of sets of environmental signals that vary with the physical location of the unit. Furthermore, the dynamic state of the neuron also determines the neurochemicals that are available in the mix. Novelty at any level greatly extends the template at that level. This creates a completely interactive environment: an action changes the environment, which changes the sensory inputs. From random data, the brain eventually will self-organize by successfully applying a method of pattern recognition. As Coward explains, "The process of thinking can be visualized as a continuously evolving group of cascades of neuron firing, extending in parallel across the hierarchical pattern extraction template (brain)."[39] This description echoes Sir Charles Scott Sherrington's earlier, albeit more poetic, description of brain activity as "a meaningful pattern though never an abiding one; a shifting harmony of subpatterns."[40]

It is difficult to summarize any system with this level of dynamic complexity. The neural condition is too internal and variable. However, Coward is a computer programmer, and programmers design systems of immense complexity out of many other simpler nested programs. While Sherrington is said to have broken with the mechanistic biologic tradition, Coward embraced it, at the same time reconfiguring it into a computational model. Operations like relational behavior, repetition, and recursion exhibited in cellular automata could start to build complexity without resorting to poetics.

The most critical aspect is that humans learn from experience, and experience configures our brains.[41] In other words, when the brain learns something, it changes. Therefore pattern and feedback—what von Neumann was missing in his cellular automata model—are intrinsic to the brain, artificial intelligence, and neuronal learning models, as they are to cybernetics, complex adaptive systems, and emergence.

Complexity is built up in two ways. Computationally the function of a neuron can be completely described by the input from other neurons, the synaptic weights (values) and the activation level or threshold of the neurons.[42] Additionally, the neuron can resend information not only back into itself but also further back to the neurons that precede it. A key feature then of the human brain is its feedback loops connecting cascade outputs back to their initiation point. These loops are commonly associated with speech and self-awareness.[43] However, this raises an important question: can feedback be construed as *relational*? Does developmental change occur in cellular automata through each cell's ability to track back, to query its neighbor's states and adjust present behavior by responding to its context? To put it another way, if we consider cellular automata as a system program, is the rule, which corresponds to relating to the neighbor state, feedback? Is this where complexity and unpredictability originate?

Neurologists surmise that simplicity can create complexity through layers of pattern recognition. The conflicting evidence is that we also know that the brain does not follow rules to make abstractions. Neurologists describe network organization, in contrast to serial algorithms, as containing neither rules nor calculation procedures. What is the relation of patterns to rules? Computational biologist Peter

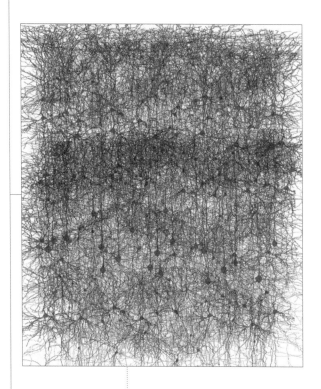

The largest and most complex part of
the human brain, the neocortex, is
shown at the cellular level. This area
generates internal processes for thought,
perception, and memory.

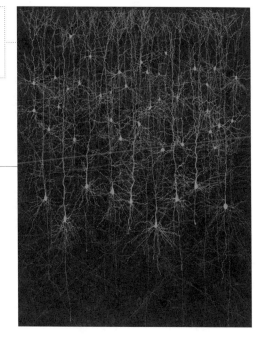

Bentley suggests that pattern is evidence of computation.[44] Therefore, the process of creating abstractions is embedded within the neuron's variable inputs and outputs—that is, it occurs spontaneously. In neuronal systems, because there is no distinction between data and program, it can be surmised that once the rule is internalized, there may be a way that patterns can relate to brains or vice versa.

Relational Architectures

> Some of the outstanding questions in genetics, evolution, and development, including notions of modularity, will involve unraveling and comprehending networks of interacting elements....Feedback makes the one-way signaling paradigm inadequate; it has been superseded by a dynamical network approach.
> —Andrew Wuensche[45]

Von Neumann saw mechanisms and logics underlying all scientific phenomena, including the human brain, while Ulam, Weiner, and Coward viewed developmental growth, random processes, and chaos as fundamental. These last three scientists postulated that feedback and cybernetics more closely modeled neurological systems. Because computational logic is not the same as the brain's logic, there is a range of opinions.[46] As of yet, it is not possible to accurately or completely model brain processes, precisely because algorithms are not the same as human thinking.

The neurologist Manfred Spitzer, however, has a modest claim: that when we learn something from even a small part of brain functioning, those findings can have potential applications even if we do not comprehend the entire system.[47] In other words, we do not need to understand the entire brain in order to understand certain features of it. And what we learn may help us to understand other processes. This has broader implications linked to formation. As Sanford Kwinter explains, "In science, natural form can be seen as an example of successfully applied principles. Through various theories of evolution and cybernetics, it is possible to understand structure as a pattern of energy and information."[48] With an informatic model, we are not looking at how rules geometrically describe form but rather as second-order controls that regulate the formation processes—that is, as a relational structural organization.[49]

While I am not suggesting that computational processes are the same as brain processes, neither am I suggesting that they are unrelated. Complexity can be built up from simple rules as long as they are relational. The structure of the cortex with its various weighted inputs and outputs filtered over six cellular layers is clearly relational. Key network features taken from Coward's model of pattern extraction describe variable, dynamic, point-to-point relationships. The very flexibility of the organization is related to the way humans learn. Some of the more exciting research being done today is John Holland's work on complex adaptive systems, extending von

Neumann's earlier questions, "Can the construction of automata by automata progress from simpler types to increasingly complicated types? Also, assuming some suitable definition of efficiency, can this evolution go from less efficient to more efficient automata?"[50] Research in artificial intelligence has developed programs that, like the brain, are capable of learning. Their principles construct what could be termed a "relational architecture" based on associations, conceptually similar to Hopfield networks or Kohonen algorithms. Simulated neural nets successfully apply the principles of pattern recognition, employed in astronomy to classify newly discovered galaxies, in machine vision, such as robotics and digital cameras, and in medicine for diagnostic testing.

New ways of conceiving space and structure require new models of organization. In this instance, cellular automata and neural networks operate as conceptual prototypes, exhibiting differential properties and relational behavior. So by studying computational biology methods, designers can not only learn to structure their models differently but also to use these new models for potential design applications. In one sense looking at cellular automata or other network models that are temporally and relationally generated affords an opportunity to view the interactive and performative aspects of design. The result is many adaptive postures of possible design solutions, instead of a single idealized solution. Before advanced computing, it was extremely difficult to model complexity. Now, however, through interdisciplinary research and time-based media, it is possible to apply different constructs and approach solutions from multiple vantage points.

What are the computational abilities of collections of cells? In biology, that question is still only partially answered. While cellular automata are not an analogy for the brain, neither are they a metaphor. The objective of network research is to extract certain principles from computational and biological models that could then frame a larger question within our current notions of formation: can simple abstract rules applied mechanistically and deterministically reproduce the unpredictable behavior of a complex natural system? The answer is yes, *but only if the rules are relational.* This investigation leads us to make some important conclusions: first, the system must be based on and exhibit a sensitivity to initial conditions (it must be non-reductive); second, in order to create unpredictable change, the rules will need to draw from neighbor-states (feedback). Both cellular automata and neuronal systems demonstrate that determinism *and* unpredictability can coexist. As the computer scientist and mathematician Rudy Rucker points out, "It might be worthwhile to think of things like flowers, thunderstorms and orgasms as computations. Yes the details of these computations may elude us, and any simulation of them would be unfeasible. Even so, there are certain properties such as unpredictability that can be usefully applied to real world phenomena."[51]

In terms of design research, relational architectures are computationally derived—that is to say, process-based in a flexible networked model. These principles have been successfully applied within various disciplines, with the closest example of relational architecture probably being those currently under investigation by Benjamin Aranda and Chris Lasch's procedural designs. In their explorations, algorithms are used to create an environment of pressures that force a design concept against, and within, issues of geometric procedure. This enables experimentation and adaptation to myriad conditions, whether programmatic or data-generated. In their experimental constructions, form and behavior emerge from processes, in the sense that every higher-level physical property (or form) can be described as a consequence of lower-level properties, with the result that when the procedural logic of cellular automata is applied consistently and deterministically, layers of code combine to generate an intricate progression of form. More recently, in collaboration with Native American basket-weaver Terroll Dew Johnson, they have extended the possibilities of cellular automata algorithms into three-dimensional spatial configurations. Theoretically the behavior of each type of cell is influenced by its simulated environment, so that when applied to material expression, this is amplified because the formal logics must interact and respond to tectonic limitations. While computationally derived, the pragmatic pressures represented by the structural potential of bark, grass, and feather produce experimental constructions of unexpected and unparalleled aesthetics.[52]

Current research by Michael Hensel, Achim Menges, and Michael Weinstock at the Architectural Association's Emergence and Design Group are also attempting to articulate the mathematical relations and interdependency of self-organizing and networked models within natural systems for architectural applications. Menges in particular is combining computational growth with associative parametric modeling to evolve differentiated surface structures. These systems employ a bottom-up logic in which all parts respond to local interactions within the environment. Because their external interactions are complex and the interpretation of the L-system is non-linear, the outcome of the growth process remains open-ended.[53]

Within experimental architectural design, Peter Testa and Devyn Weiser, founders of the Emergent Design Group at MIT, have developed new computational design methods and open source software such as Agency GP, Genr8, and Weaver.[54] As part of Testa & Weiser's Los Angeles–based research practice, their software demonstrates reflexive structures through the integration of non-linear control models and AI constraint settings. In particular, Weaver exemplifies a new type of agential-materialist combinatorics that supports simulation of emergent structural morphology and robotic fabrication of architectural form.

Just as von Neumann, Ulam, and Coward reflected on biologic processes to extend the possibilities of computational design, so design research can learn from complex natural systems. The task today for designers is to articulate the mathematics and processes that are potentially useful, both from a cognitive viewpoint as well as for possible design applications. This however will require sustained research in order to apply the principles and dynamics of organization that natural systems exhibit and artificially constructed systems can use.

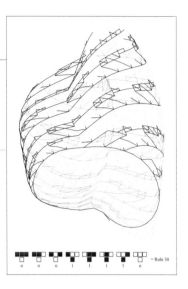

This initial set of experiments by Aranda/Lasch employs a cellular program to produce a weave across a shape that is defined by a distribution of points or nodes. This results in complex weaves because the algorithm is automatically feeding information back into itself to make the next decision. The relational weave adjusts and adapts as it travels over a surface.

Achim Menges: Fibrous Surfaces
Recent experiments investigate the possibilities of combining computational growth and associative parametric modeling to evolve a differentiated surface structure consisting of a dense network of interlocking members from a basic array of simple straight elements. A variable distribution-algorithm derived from GENR8 establishes a network of lines on the surface indicating the position of each element and the related node type. Instances of the generic parametric component then populate the system accordingly.

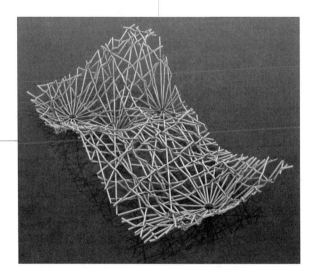

Within this framework, it is then possible to view cellular automata and neural networks as models of emergence. To understand organization, we need to understand the coarse-grained rules and relations for joining cells/units, components and assemblies, which inform a global geometry. Although complex geometries of contemporary tectonics must begin from mathematics, to be operationally valid they must also respond to context. Through the study of computational and biological models, we can begin to understand the extremely important role of contextual feedback on structured pattern in morphology. This in itself predicts dialogic possibilities for an autopoietic architecture, defined as "a machine organized...as a network of processes of production (transformation and destruction) of components which through their interactions and transformations continuously regenerate and realize the network of processes (relations) that produced them."[55] A relational architecture therefore means adjusting and extending the parameters of an algorithmic system beyond structural performance, to make it more inclusive by enfolding environmental social/cultural performance conditions as well. Only by including neighboring conditions within a network organization based on feedback can such a relational architecture be achieved. In whatever form relational architecture evolves in the future, as it stands, it is informational and predicated on a dynamic internal structure and organization. Form-finding as such is clearly not the objective, but instead instantiates a deterministic unfolding of an unpredictable and variable process.

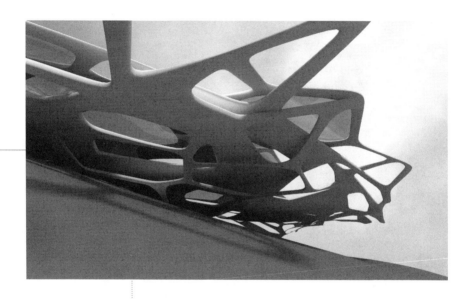

Jun Yu: *Forms of Cellular Aggregation*
(2005)
Instructors: Marcelo Spina, Peter Testa:
SCI-Arc 2GBX Studio
GENR8 (Generative Form Modeling and
Manufacturing) is a surface modeling
program that involves artificial
intelligence and complex feedback loops.
It is based on natural growth systems
within a dynamic shaping environment/
infrastructure and a localized application
of automated processes.

Notes

....

1...Alfred North Whitehead, *Process and Reality: An Essay in Cosmology*, corrected edition, eds. David Ray Griffin and Donald W. Sherburne (New York: Free Press, 1978).

2...Ibid.

3...Kostas Terzidis, "Algorithmic Architecture" (lecture, Harvard Graduate School of Design, Sept. 21, 2005).

4...Arthur Eddington, *The Harvest of a Quiet Eye*, ed. A. L. Mackay (Bristol and London: Institute of Physics, 1977), 50.

5...John von Neumann, "The First Draft Report on the EDVAC (Electronic Discrete Variable Automatic Calculator)," contract no. W-670-ORD-4926, between the United States Army Ordinance Department and the University of Pennsylvania Moore School of Electrical Engineering, University of Pennsylvania, June 30, 1945.

6...John von Neumann, "The General and Logical Theory of Automata," in Zenon W. Pylyshyn, ed., *Perspectives on the Computer Revolution* (Englewood Cliffs, New Jersey: Prentice-Hall, 1970).

7...Ibid. See also Rudy Rucker and John Walker, *Exploring Cellular Automata* (San Rafael, CA: Autodesk, 1989).

8...Von Neumann, "The General and Logical Theory of Automata," 315.

9...Rucker and Walker, *Exploring Cellular Automata*.

10...Jeffrey Kipnis posed the question as a radical alterity: how can something have identity and yet still be different from itself? "The Necessary Difference between Identity and the Same" (presentation address, Congress CATH, University of Leeds, Bradford, UK, July 10, 2004).

11...William Aspray, *John von Neumann and the Origins of Modern Computing* (Cambridge, MA: MIT Press, 1990), 204.

12...Jean-Pierre Protzen, "Design Theories and Methods" (lecture, University of California Berkeley, April 10, 2003).

13...Originally the term "computer" referred to a person who performed numerical calculations, usually with the aid of a mechanical calculating device or analog computer, most often women with degrees in calculus. Wendy Hui Kyong Chun, "On Software, or the Persistence of Visual Knowledge," *Grey Room* 18 (Winter 2005): 26–51.

14...John Holland, "Outline for a Logical Theory of Adaptive Systems," in Arthur W. Burks, ed., *Essays on Cellular Automata* (Urbana: University of Illinois Press, 1970), 287, 350–51.

15...Ibid., 53–54.

16...Stephen Wolfram, *A New Kind of Science* (Champaign, IL: Wolfram Media, 2002).

17...Steve I. Heims, *John von Neumann and Norman Weiner: From Mathematics to the Technologies of Life and Death* (Cambridge, MA: MIT Press, 1982). Von Neumann was also responsible for the interdisciplinary atmosphere at Princeton where he introduced Alan Turing to Alonzo Church; the two collaborated on the "mathematical theory of recursive functions," or The Church Turing thesis.

18...Rucker and Walker, *Exploring Cellular Automata*.

19...Stanislaw Ulam, "On Some Mathematical Problems Connected with Patterns of Growth of Figures," *Proceedings of Symposia in Applied Mathematics* 14 (Providence, RI: American Mathematics Society, 1962): 215–24.

20...Stanislaw Ulam and John von Neumann, *Theory of Self-Reproduction Automata*, ed. Arthur Burks (Urbana: University of Illinois Press, 1966), 77.

21...Stanislaw Ulam, "Random Processes and Transformations," in *Stanislaw Ulam: Sets, Numbers and Universes* (Cambridge, MA: MIT Press, 1974), 326–37.

22...Aspray, *John von Neumann and the Origins of Modern Computing*, 201.

23...Ibid.

24...Ibid.

25...Norbert Weiner, *Cybernetics and Control and Communication in the Animal and the Machine* (Cambridge, MA: MIT Press, 1948).

26...John von Neumann, *The Computer and the Brain* (New Haven and London: Yale University Press, 1958).

27...Outside of mathematics, it is not well known that most of our mathematical tools, from simple arithmetic through differential calculus to algebraic topologies, rely on the assumption of linearity. John Holland, *Hidden Order* (New York: Basic Books, 1995), 15.

28...Ulam, "Random Processes and Transformations."

29...John Holland, *Hidden Order*, 15.

30...Eugene P. Wigner, "Are We Machines?" *Proceedings of the American Philosophical Society* 113, no. 2 (Apr. 17, 1969): 95–101.

31...Manfred Spitzer, *The Mind within the Net: Models of Learning, Thinking, and Acting* (Cambridge, MA: MIT Press, 1999), 23.

32...L. Andrew Coward, "The Pattern Extraction Hierarchy Architecture: A Connectionist Alternative to the von Neumann Architecture," in Jose Mira, Roberto Morenzo-Diaz, and Joan Cabestanz, eds., *Biological and Artificial Computation: From Neuroscience to Technology* (Berlin: Springer, 1997), 634–43.

33...L. Andrew Coward, *Pattern Thinking* (New York: Praeger, 1990).

34...Ibid., 59–61. Sensory input to action is also referring to behaviorism, a psychological approach based on theory that behavior can be studied and explained scientifically without recourse to internal mental states.

35...Floyd Ratliff, "Complex Dynamic Behaviour of a Real Neural Network in terms of a few Simple Basic Principles," in Eduardo R. Caianiello, ed., *On Fields of Inhibitory Influence in a Neural Network* (New York: Springer-Verlag, 1968).

36...http://www.medterms.com/script/main/art.asp?articlekey=25283 (accessed Sept. 4, 2006).

37...Coward, *Pattern Thinking*.

38...Ibid., 3, 6–9. These are Coward's definitions:

 I. A pattern is something that repeats; i.e. wallpaper in space; the phases of the moon in time. A pattern is a set of components, each of which is a set of patterns.

 II. Pattern as hierarchy: The component of complex patterns is generally relatively simple and are themselves composed of even more simple patterns, i.e. nesting.

 III. A component can indicate positively or negatively for the presence of a pattern. An individual pattern may be only a convenient and efficient step in reaching a high complexity pattern from simple inputs and may have no significance beyond that.

 IV. The degree of indication can vary between components. Recursive operations may have the result of variance. A pattern repeats when the weighted sum of the identified components exceeds a threshold.

 V. The recognition of a complex pattern can be interpreted on a system level as an action recommendation: this pattern is present, therefore do that. How we can guess what to do in a novel situation.

39...Ibid., 66, 114.

40...Charles S. Sherrington, *Man on his Nature: The Gifford Lectures, Edinburgh* (Cambridge: Cambridge University Press, 1940), 178.

41...Spitzer, *The Mind within the Net*, 37.

42...Ibid., 23.

43...Manfred Spitzer suggests that less than .5 brain activity is devoted to external input and output, the rest is all interior processes. To put it another way, 99.5 of all brain activity is an internal conversation. As Spitzer succinctly explains, "The brain is only concerned with itself." The evidence that the chemicals surrounding the synaptic connections are also affected by the content of the synaptic activity itself verifies this notion. See Spitzer, *The Mind within the Net*, 169.

44...Peter Bentley, email correspondence with the author, June 12, 2006.

45...Andrew Wuensche, "Basins of Attraction in Network Dynamics: A Conceptual Framework for Biomolecular Networks," in *Modularity in Developmental Evolution*. (Chicago: University of Chicago Press, 2004), 288.

46...See Peter Bentley's essay "Climbing through Complexity Ceilings," in this volume.

47...Spitzer, *The Mind within the Net*, 1–2.

48...Sanford Kwinter, "Thinking about Architecture" (lecture, Massachusetts Institute of Technology, Sept. 26, 2005).

49...Ibid.

50...Von Neumann and Burks, eds., "The Theory of Self-reproducing Automata," 92.

51...Rucker and Walker, *Exploring Cellular Automata*.

52...Benjamin Aranda and Chris Lasch, *Pamphlet Architecture 27: Tooling* (New York: Princeton Architectural Press, 2006). Aranda/Lasch and Johnson's collaboration was exhibited at Artists Space: Architecture and Design in New York (2006).

53...Achim Menges, email correspondence with the author, July 27, 2006.

54...See Peter Testa and Devyn Weiser, "Material Agency," in this volume.

55...The full quotation from Maturana and Varela includes autopoietic as "(ii) constitute it (the machine) as a concrete unity in space in which they (the components) exist by specifying the topological domain of its realization as such a network." Humberto Maturana and Francisco Varela, *Autopoietic Systems* (Urbana, IL: Biological Computer Lab Report, 1973), 78.

Scalar Networks, Super Creeps: Approaching the Non-Standard in the Architecture of Servo

Christopher Hight

> …behold the breaking down of a world that has erased its borders: fainting away.
> –Julia Kristeva, *The Powers of Horror*

Every quaint suburban home, banal big-box retail store, kitsch shopping mall, and generic office building contains a small cybernetic interface that allows them to exist and links each into a vast and paranoid networking of subjects, machines, natural processes, and social spaces. We call it a thermostat. Norbert Weiner explained the core principle of cybernetics, feedback, through the example of the thermostat since the technology is so familiar.[1] A human operator simply moves a lever that calibrates a laminated strip of metal that bends according to its temperature, triggering a circuit that turns on the air-conditioner, which in turn alters the temperature until the strip of metal bends back and opens the circuit again. This example of negative feedback is reassuringly domestic, literally comforting to unreconstructed humanists. It suggests nothing really changed with the advent of cybernetics, that in fact everything, including our enclosed spaces of domesticity and subjectivity, will remain exactly in home-o-stasis (sic). In the decades that have passed, the reality of the built environment based on thermostatic control is less placid. For the thermostat regulated a closed system (a closed envelope of a house) but is linked into a grid of energy consumption, distribution, and production, and therefore the political ecologies that determine our future. Like a giant cellular automata in which the dumb on-and-off states of individual cells interact to produce global patterns, the simple cycling of a billion independently set thermostats contribute to emergent effects: electrical grids fail, ice caps melt, governments are toppled, civilizations rise and fall. The thermostatically regulated architectural enclosure is a diagram for a molecular social order in which discrete feedback loops cycle on and off in solipsistic bliss.

Shortly after Weiner's thermostatic cybernetics, Reyner Bahnam argued that proliferating air conditioning, plumbing, and lighting systems in architecture, and by extension, the city, had effectively transformed the objects of architectural and urban knowledge.[2] The "well-tempered environment" had replaced the cavelike and discrete bodylike typologies known to architecture with something more analogous to the nomadic campfire and its gradients of heat and light. The city was no longer composed of static monuments but homeostatic systems that, if properly regulated, Banham implied, might allow different forms of social and political life to arise. Yet, Banham argued, architects' obsession with the construction of clear borders and discrete artifacts often prevented the discipline from dealing with this new gradient and radiant reality as a source of design innovation.[3]

Of course today we would add the electronic and telecommunications infrastructures that Bahnam oddly downplayed even for his time. Peer-to-peer networks, distributed computing, open-source movements, satellite televangelism, cell phone–organized protest movements, and other forms of information network–enabled communities are raising challenges to legal and social structures of liberal democracies. Information infrastructures and intelligent sensing systems are now being unleashed from their domestic servitude as thermostats, electric door openers, and alarm systems, and are beginning to establish ubiquitous ambient computing as the replacement for what used to be called urbanism.

How do we give a figure to such a reality? How might architects operate at this level of networked intensity? Not by repeating architectural and urban typologies and concepts of space as a problem of containment and boundaries, or even by trying to operate in the sorts of spaces and sites these provide.

I would argue that servo's architecture, increasingly constructed of tubes, conduits for circuits, snaking coils, and chases, suggests an alternative approach where social territories, like the organization of the firm itself, are defined by software firewalls and signal strength; public space has been displaced by propriety Wi-Fi hotspots and community is supplemented by network propinquity without necessarily physical proximity.

Servo does not "hot desk" so much as "hot city." Their "office" is physically dispersed across three to four cites at any given moment and constructed on the fly through the network infrastructures of the global information economy. While architects often brag about their frequent flyer miles, usually these globetrotters are tethered to a rather large base where minions receive instructions like missals from an absent god. For servo there is no central hub, only the proliferation of consultants and fabricators. Their proximity is measured not by distance but by baud

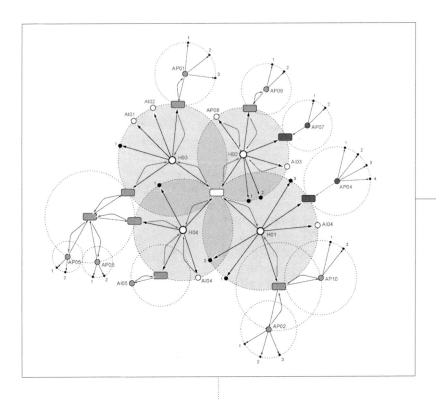

Aaron White, diagram of servo's practice, 2006.

servo, Thermocline, 2002. Thermocline upgrades the infrastructure of a conventional furniture unit, transforming its primarily tactile interface of surface-to-body into a multisensory user atmosphere. The Emonic Environment, Thermocline's computational architecture, is an artificial neural network of sound, lighting, and computing systems. An array of sound sensors distributed throughout the gallery collect residual conversation as a byproduct of the exhibition environment. This sonic material is then distributed to a central computer to be processed by custom software, which uses algorithms to transform the incoming sonic information into sets of new sound patterns that are then distributed into Thermocline's speaker network, ultimately triggering its LED lighting array.

Graphic Notation

○ Architectural Design
◉ Interaction and Information Systems
● Automated Manufacturing
▭ Shared Technology 1: Design Software
▬ Shared Technology 2: Interaction and Information Systems
▬ Shared Technology 3: Automated Manufacturing
— Uni-Directional Collaboration
▽ Multi-Directional Collaboration (incorporating feedback)

⊙ Practice Envelope
Practice Identity

Textual Notation

H   servo Hub
AI   Affiliated Institution
AP   Affiliated Practice
H01   Los Angeles Hub
H02   Stockholm Hub
H03   New York Hub
H04   Zurich Hub

Affiliated Institutions / Practices

AI01   Cornell University
AI02   Pratt Institute
AI03   KTH / Royal Institute of Technology
AI04   UCLA
AI05   ETH
AP0   Responsive Systems Group
AP0   SKDP
AP0   Small Design Firm
AP0   Warner Brothers Studios
AP0   MIT Media Lab
AP0   Interactive Institute / Smart Studio
AP0   Caran
AP08   Krets
AP09   Casey Reas

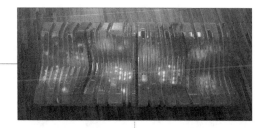

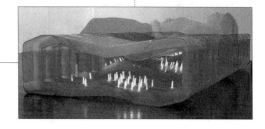

rates. They describe their practice not in terms of discrete projects but as "product lines," in which each commission is an experiment within a trajectory of research. Even the name references something that is less a discrete thing than a conduit and transducer of information or intensity. Servo has begun the task of mobilizing network feedback as a platform for innovating the nature of practice, the nature of the objects of that practice, the site for their designs, and as a business model.

Moreover, servo's projects increasingly map the organization of their practice. Early projects operated at the interface between bodies—human and architectural. For example, Thermocline seems more or less a molded plastic couch with electronic augmentation that would respond to the location of a user, altering the lighting and heat, and therefore create a feedback network of stimuli between the body of the user and surface. Similarly, in Lobbi-ports, what were essentially hybrids between a lobby and an elevator cab would move across the structural frame of a tower, reconfiguring the circulation and program and signaling these by peristaltic movement of the building skin. While operating at different scales, in both of these projects discrete bodies mapped, responded, and deterritorialized another. In Lobbi-ports, the well-known and unified typology of the tower, a body of sorts, becomes an network of social relations because of the interaction between smaller prosthetics. In Thermocline, the ergonomic/functional typology of a human body and furniture is transformed into an ambient field of intensity at the interface between the plastic and fleshy skin of its components. The interactions between the local physical and the phenomenal effect and global systems of information management produced a networked organization as an effect.

Just as Theromocline employed feedback mechanisms based on intensity of heat and light, Lattice Archpelogics can be read as the dispersion of Bahnam's and Weiner's thermostatic controls into a distributed field, in which multiple feedback loops between the sensing pods and circuits and subjects create not homeostasis but recursive pulsations far from equilibrium. In their Vibronic Environments proposal, the existing walled courtyard of P.S.1 is turned into a campsite for urban nomads reclining on mats (designed by bio(t)hing), clustered like barnacles around islands formed where conduits of services, wired and unwired, converge. The users can "jack in" to the music or surf for information, and their occupation and use in turn alters the experience of other users and the global conditioning of the space itself via light, watery mists, and sound. The tribal elder that sat near the center of the proverbial fire is here replaced by the DJ; the hearth by the mixing table. The project is notably sparse rather than congested, referencing a world where one no longer needs to be physically adjacent to be part of the scene; however, their images also suggest a certain lonely, almost desert condition. Unless one is sitting on the mats and jacked in, there is simply isolation. That is to say, proximity but no propinquity.

Here another transformation can be detected in regards to the lifeworlds that servo's projects engage. Previously the projects presented and evoked a rather clinical, benign vision of the networked society. This tendency toward a cheerful

servo, Vibronic Environments, 2004.
Conceived as an augmented environment, the
system's physical architecture grows and
accumulates throughout the space of the
courtyard, resembling a thickened surface
or mat. Embedded into its acrylic surfaces
is a responsive network of lighting and
vibrotactile technologies that activate
the physical architecture with real-
time-processed information. Incoming
sonic information is transformed into a
series of remixes distributed throughout
the architecture's surfaces in the form
of programmable LEDs and inaudible
vibrations.

servo, in collaboration with Small Design
Firm, Lobbi-ports, 2002.
The curtain wall is transformed into
a dynamic lighting membrane via an
algorithmically controlled network of
activity sensors, visual monitors,
computer-processing infrastructures,
and the skin's own external lighting
system. The result is the formation of
a responsive communications network,
allowing the building to observe its
own internal programmatic activity and
register the effects of that activity
in the form of lighting patterns on the
exterior.

interpretation of networked culture and post-Fordism is a common trait of "non-standard" or digitally oriented architectural practices, which often convey the same sort of boosterism found in *Wired* magazine. The infinite formal variation promised by mass-customization and the performative fluctuation of responsive environment is often accepted as the natural expression of a zeitgeist, a smooth space of radical-ized capital in which information is simply exchange mechanisms, an architecture of consumer choice. That is to say, the network society is routinely presented not simply as signaling a transformation but as libratory or even "revolutionary." Yet this can just as easily tend toward an extreme solipsism, for example in Nicholas Negroponte's prediction that newspapers would be curated by individual taste, meaning on the one hand more choice, and on the other a tendency toward ho-meostatic positive feedback as what we take for reality becomes a reflection of "the daily Me."[3]

In servo's most recent projects, an unease has emerged about this tendency. The projects are darker in title, in effects, and in concept. For example, The Gene-alogy of Speed project is ostensibly designed to display the same Nike shoes that are talismans of global capital. The shoes are held in a network of conduits and capsules that conflate the connotations of banal experience and fantastical horror: the everyday pneumatics of banking machines meet the fantasical egg pods of a Geiger-designed *Alien* film. If the evocation of special effects–based films seems prob-lematic, it is worth remembering that it was architecture and not the cinema screen that was the original site of the special effect and its libidinal powers. The spatial effects of Baroque church evoked the ecstatic but also fear.[5] The sci-fi overtones seem placeholders for research just beginning in these works. It has been a while since an architect overtly championed the creepy or the horrifying; the last time was with Peter Eisenman's deconstruction and Greg Lynn's early texts on folding. However, these operated through representational strategies that positioned the monstrous as a deviation from a normative architectural body of knowledge. Monster movies operate by retracing identity and representation, while horror, real horror, concerns revealing the limits of their possibility. There is always a tension in servo's work between the operative and the representational. My argument here is a problemati-zation and mobilization of this potential.

This transformation is perhaps more than a shift in tone, but rather begins to engage a heretofore overlooked aspect of the network culture within architecture: that its power derives from a certain sense of horror. Bahnam's primordial campfire was of course dependent upon a European spatial imagination and orientalism, in which the "poetics of fire" are embedded within a site that at once suggests the nor-mative anchor of societal order of hearth and home and the instrument of witch-craft. In our Promethean myths of the origin of culture, the campfire is a liminal threshold, on the one hand marking humanity's emergence from animalistic in-stinct, but also an ur-technology that dangerously gives humanity powers it cannot tame and which seem to upset the natural order of things. It is both an instrument

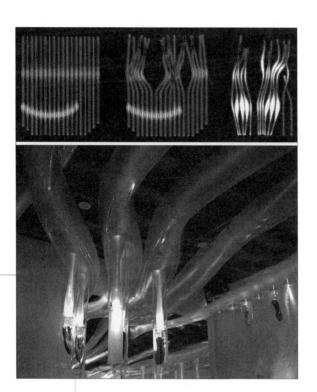

servo, in collaboration with SKDP and
Karen Kimmel, The Genealogy of Speed,
2004. The exhibition infrastructure
incorporates fiber-optic lighting
technology and vacuum-formed acrylic panel
systems exploring the resonance between
material and informational systems.
The display system is reconfigurable,
incorporating aspects of "speed" at an
operative scale as well as a thematic one.

for the purifications of power and science and the catalyst for the categorical transgressions of alchemy, a symbol of entropic dissolution of what were considered proper boundaries and borders of existence.

Information technology intensifies the connectivity of networks by converting all content into intensities of energy, electric, thermal, or bio-chemical. This allows exchange of content but blurs what were once thought of as discrete domains or categories. Indeed, the discourses surrounding networking and globalization invoke a plethora of tropes about the erasure of border: smoothness, free markets, spaces of flows, networking itself. While these are usually couched in terms of a technological liberation, this must be understood as the displacement of the organic-architectonic model of the organism by the discovery that evolutionary processes are mediated by the electro-chemical energy stored as molecular organizations and transmitted via feedback loops of selection, recombination, mutation, and transmission (i.e., genetics and evolutionary biology). In this model, as the historian Georges Canguilhem claimed, "life is the production, transmission and reception of information," and knowledge is "nothing more than methods for moving things around and changing the [network of] relations among objects and subjects," while the theorist of computation Freidrich Kittler relates that in computers "everything becomes number: imageless, soundless, wordless quantity" but really everything becomes electrical potential (on or off)—if you own a recent laptop, heat.[6] Life is no longer about extensive forms and geometries but intensities of energy and its transmission. In what amounts to a cybernetic metaphysics, this electro-chemical model of life eschews architectonic and spatial geometries inherent in the organic model of the body in favor of topology for the simple reason that the organic unity of "bodies" are merely vehicles for transmission of information, which in turn is merely stored energy.

This intensive dissolution of corporal containment as a meaningful boundary, and of its prosthetic extension as enclosed spaces of buildings, suggests a psychoanalytic reversion to the oceanic sense of continuity experienced by the infantile subject before individuation of the body from the world begins. For Julia Kristeva, the dissolution of borders, corporal or territorial, is necessarily the affect of abjection.[7] The abject was more than a version of the sublime, for while the sublime ultimately allows the subject to encompass that which threatens it, the abject triggers that moment of primal sublimation of the non-object worlds into the separations that constitute the subject.[8] Ralph Ellison's Invisible Man, for example, recounts a dream of a young African American girl whose body dissolves into ectoplasm in a culture that refused to acknowledge her; Deleuze described masochism as the desire for the disassembly of the self while the purpose of interrogation techniques of psychological (and physical) torture is, in part, the dissolving of the sense of self.[9] Thus, the libratory aspects of such dissolution may seem liberating and empowering for those most able to negotiate the surf, but this depends on who holds the power and desires the dissolution.

Yet the discourses of mass-customization and even emergence that now preoccupy architecture can be read as attempts to sublimate these problems in order to conserve architecture as a coherent body of knowledge. Many of the architects who pay lip service to the so-called digital revolution produce objects that, however convoluted their forms, occupy the entirely conventional ideas of site and typologies of the city. Others are content to make monuments to infrastructure, fetishizing the box rather than the information projected through it. However, the task of architecture today is not about making architecture that resembles a body without organs (a protoplasm) but of assembling organs without the now-empty frockcoat that we call "Architecture."

These matters come to a head in servo's <u>Dark Places</u>, designed for an exhibition curated by Joshua Decter at the Santa Monica Museum of Art. The project provides a spatial display interface for the work of seventy-five other architects. A series of conduit-like forms converge into nodes that hold informational interfaces, and then bloom in arching trajectories suspended in space and terminated by translucent screens onto which work is projected, organized according to eight linked sequences. Not unlike the Eames' exhibition design for the IBM Corporate Exhibit Center in 1971, servo's project is at once part of the exhibit and a spatial armature for the work on display, and thus mediates between the curatorial content and the experience of that content by the user both cognitively and as affect. However, while the Eameses attempted to provide a reassuring armature for historical representation, servo's interface is projective and unsettling.

On the one hand, Dark Places continues servo's explorations of the relationship between space, information, and the subject using latticelike forms. It has some similarity to <u>Lattice Archipelogic's</u> use of networked lighting, here the lights becoming media content. However, the clean and ordered cloudlike filigree of Lattice Archipelogics reemerges in Dark Places as if they were wrenched, warped, and pulled like taffy. As a result, the typical typologies of media installations (partitions, tables, screens) are incorporated into a network of lines, of necks, that do not interact so much and entwine the subject. Again, there is a certain effect of horror—David Cronenberg meets *Little Shop of Horrors*. But here it is taken to a further level of exploration. The Lattice project's grid, whose lights playfully blinked a dance with the viewer in geometric purity, has become distorted, like a straining, screaming head of a Francis Bacon crucifixion. Rather than serving as simply an empty backdrop, here the black box of the gallery participates in the work—perhaps for the first time in servo's work. The normative architecture plays a similar role as Bacon's cubic prisms did for his figures, providing a frame that at once intensifies the object and which concentrates the subject into its monstrous expression. The otherwise taut surfaces are also inscribed with scars of cable conduits. This is not an architecture of smoothly NURBS-driven or algorithmically generated utopia or emergent formal complexity, but a violence of geometry. The user does not look at the work from an outside position, in elevation, but almost as in section. The cut ends of the lattice hold the backlit screens that recall the nodes of the Lattice but are no longer twinkling like a thousand points of light. The nodes, these corpuscles, have been ripped

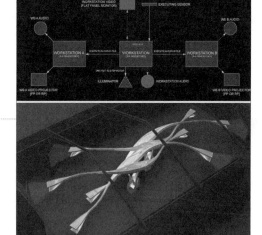

servo, Dark Places, 2006. Functioning less as a passive display and lighting system, the design infrastructure provides an active and dynamic spatial instrument for the absorption, filtration, and synthesis of interaction between gallery users and the material on display. Movement patterns, communication activity, and other forms of physical and informational use are monitored, or mapped, by a network of intelligent technologies embedded into the infrastructure's material surfaces. These use patterns are then used as inputs in order to generate new spatial effects through sound, lighting, and image technologies.

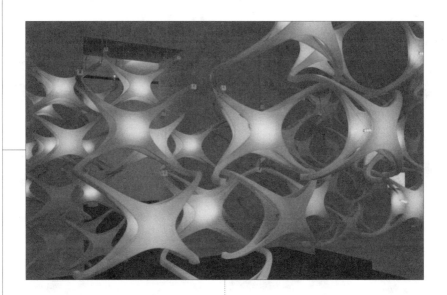

servo, Lattice Archipelogics [see also
next spread]

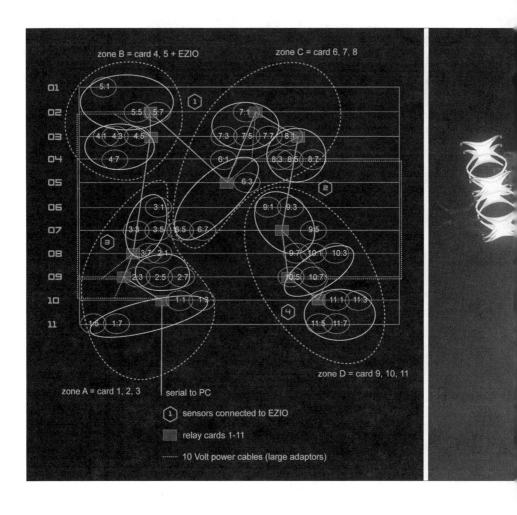

zone B = card 4, 5 + EZIO   zone C = card 6, 7, 8

01
02
03
04
05
06
07
08
09
10
11

5:1
5:5 5:7
4:1 4:3 4:5
4:7
7:1
7:3 7:5 7:7 8:1
6:1
8:3 8:5 8:7
6:3
3:1
9:1 9:3
3:3 3:5 6:5 6:7
9:5
3:7 2:1
9:7 10:1 10:3
2:3 2:5 2:7
10:5 10:7
1:1 1:3
11:1 11:3
1:5 1:7
11:5 11:7

zone D = card 9, 10, 11

zone A = card 1, 2, 3   serial to PC

☐ sensors connected to EZIO

■ relay cards 1-11

------ 10 Volt power cables (large adaptors)

servo, Lattice Archipelogics, 2002.
Lattice Archipelogics is an interior-
scale installation that integrates remote
sensing and lighting technology to explore
the resonance between material systems
and their distributional and indexical
capacities. Motion sensors track the
circulation of visitors moving through the
installation; these patterns of movement
are then processed by organizing them into
cellular particles that are distributed
in variable, algorithmically driven
assemblies, triggering an LED lighting
array.

open like blisters, their information content radiating out into the dark room, and in this gaping yawn a ghostly image of another world appears, pulses, fades, and shimmers.

Thus, servo's most recent work suggests a shift from focusing on innovating the object of architecture to reconfiguring its subject: the redistribution of borders of the discipline into the power structures of the networked economy. Needless to say, for many architects this might be terrifying in that it raises questions as to the status of the object as architecture, as well as the nature of the practice of architecture. Luckily for them, all this seems to occur in the safest of sites: the gallery—never mind that the gallery exhibit and attendant media has served as the laboratory for architectural innovation since there was such a thing as modern architecture. However, in a networked knowledge economy, where everything has become in a real sense a problem of design, the gallery is not a site for disinterested aesthetic representation so much as a potential place for production of community, of knowledge, and perhaps of fleeting subjective affect. Servo's projects give a figure for, and make new sub-clusters within, the semi-choreographed conduits of gradient intensities that effuse our spatial and social experience. While thus far these take the form of installations and exhibitions, these projects are also distillations of our present and prototypes for future practices of truly intensive architects that may, finally, radiate more heat than skillfully sculpt forms in light, digital or otherwise. Servo might represent the last generation of modern architects, serving as conduits of that which is replacing us.

Notes

....

Epigraph: Julia Kristeva, *The Powers of Horror* (New York: Columbia University Press, 1982), 4.

1...Norbert Weiner, *Cybernetics*, 2nd ed. (Cambridge, MA: MIT Press, 1965), 96.

2...Reyner Banham, *The Architecture of the Well Tempered Environment*, 2nd ed. (Chicago: University of Chicago Press, 1969), 44.

3...Ibid., 311–12.

4...Nicholas Negroponte, *Being Digital* (New York: Vintage, 1995), 152–54.

5...Norman M. Klein, *The Vatican to Vegas: A History of Special Effects* (New York: The New Press, 2004).

6...Georges Canguilhem, *A Vital Rationalist* (New York: Zone Books, 1994), 319; and Freidrich Kittler, *Gramophone Film Typewriter* (Stanford, CA: Stanford University Press, 1999).

7...Julia Kristeva, *The Powers of Horror*, 1–17; 53–55; 59–67.

8...Ibid., 9–11.

9...Ralph Ellison, *The Invisible Man* (New York: Vintage, 1995), 7; Gilles Deleuze and Félix Guattari, *A Thousand Plateaus* (Minneapolis: University of Minneapolis Press, 1987), 151–53; and Elaine Scarry, *The Body in Pain* (New York: Oxford University Press, 1985), 47–48.

Stop Motion Studies

David Crawford

In-Network

The United States health care system uses the terms "in-network" and "out-of-network" to refer to relationships that exist between insurance companies and doctors. For instance, while physician A may be in-network for me and out-of-network for you, our insurance plans may stipulate just the opposite in regard to physician B; assuming of course, that we are not among the 45 million Americans who are uninsured altogether.[1]

While doctors may be beyond the reach of our bodies, our minds are all in-network when it comes to media. The consolidation of media companies[2] and the explosion of distribution channels (cable and the internet) means that we as consumers, "targets" in advertising-speak, are delivered up to corporate interests on an unprecedented scale. We as citizens have also benefited from the net's decentralized architecture, yet if we ever thought we stood to gain something more than a paycheck from pouring our blood, sweat, and tears into it, now would appear to be the moment of truth.

With attacks on net neutrality on one side and warrantless wiretaps on the other, the net is increasingly under attack as a site of consciousness-raising and political action.[3] Should the balance tip in favor of a corporatism that defines us as targets rather than civilians, we may come to view the net in a primarily Orwellian light. What was once a heterotopic[4] digital commons could just as easily become an always-on panopticon. How are we to preserve our identities as citizens?

If we are to be a "we" and not simply an "I," we must inhabit places that provide a context for the "we"—as in "We the People"—to both recognize each other and make our voices heard.[5] While the street is the prototypical site for the promotion of collective identity and formation of protest, its vibrancy has waned in the face of a network of privatized interests, which have denuded its human potential in favor of the needs of automobiles. Despite the "we" of the street yielding to the "I" of my car, there remains a second site capable of sustaining collective self-awareness in public transit.

Meanwhile, the attacks of 3/11 (Madrid), 7/7 (London), and 7/11 (Mumbai) have demonstrated a concerted effort to strike fear into the hearts of citizens who (by necessity or choice) continue to participate in the "we-ness" this form of urbanity affords. It is not without significance that through these terrifying image-events,[6] a shared architectural space of mutual self-interest becomes horribly refracted before being fed back to an "I," who invariably sits alone in front of a screen. Will the

"SMS-8," *Stop Motion Studies*, 2002-2004

architecture of the future consist only of MySpace, or can we rescue and protect something we might call our space?

The Body Politic

From 2002 to 2004, I produced thirteen installments of an artwork entitled the *Stop Motion Studies (SMS)*. At first largely formal works exploring digital chronophotography and the subway, they have taken on new meaning amid the war on civilians.[7] While the *SMS* project tends to be described in terms of its immateriality, this was never an entirely satisfying paradigm. To call it "net art" is to suggest that there is such a thing as "non-networked art," despite the ubiquity of the net as the underlying architecture of our culture.

Instead, I have preferred to interpret the project from either a cinematographic standpoint—that is, in terms of the relation these algorithmically generated animations have to the history of the moving image; or alternatively, from the standpoint of its socio-political bearing. Looked at from a cinematographic point of view, some relevant questions become: What happens phenomenologically in the time between two images in a sequence? How can algorithmic montage enable us to see in new ways?

Placing an emphasis upon the *SMS* project's pre- and post-cinematic ambitions suggests that while its language is network specific, it remains a form of network practice that takes the net for granted. Regardless, perhaps it is time to push the net-specific and cinematographic frameworks into the background and instead foreground the way the project provides a window into the vitality of the subway. This, in the face of an unrelenting stream of images that present public transport as a place where bodies are eviscerated and lives cut short.

As I grew up in the suburbs, I was in a unique position to appreciate the subway. Not surprisingly, I found a humanity absent in the shopping malls. While being elbow-to-elbow with strangers can sometimes be unpleasant and even dangerous on the rare occasion, this is also part of what it means to belong to a society; nothing ventured, nothing gained. Conversely, I have seen drivers treat others in ways they would never consider if they were not behind the wheel of a car (being shielded by metal and glass changes you).

One hermeneutic approach to art-making is to see it as a tool. Looked at in this light, it becomes possible to view its production as a dialectic with a unique potential to reveal, instruct, and inspire. For the artist, some relevant questions then become: What is this work showing me that I had not seen before? How can I augment the effect of this tool to maximize its potential? In this regard, the *SMS* project has shown me at least two things. First, belonging to a society means belonging to it with your body. Second, it is time to step from behind our screens and re-inhabit our citizen bodies before we forget how to be more than consumers. Ironically, this may be the only way to save the net.

Notes

1... "Income, Poverty, and Health Insurance Coverage in the United States: 2004" (U.S. Census Bureau, Aug. 2005), http://www.census.gov/prod/2005pubs/p60-229.pdf (accessed July 15, 2006).

2... Peter Ahlberg, "The National Entertainment State, 2006," *The Nation* (July 3, 2006), http://www.thenation.com/doc/20060703/mediachart (accessed July 15, 2006).

3... On net neutrality, see "Save the Internet: Frequently Asked Questions," http://www.savetheinternet.com/=faq (accessed July 15, 2006). For a refresher on the NSA warrantless wiretaps, see "The NSA Warrantless Domestic Surveillance," EFF (Electronic Frontier Foundation), http://www.eff.org/Privacy/Surveillance/NSA (accessed July 15, 2006).

4... Michel Foucault, "Of Other Spaces," trans. Jay Miskowiec, http://foucault.info/documents/heteroTopia (accessed July 15, 2006).

5... Rebecca Solnit, "Democracy Should be Exercised Regularly, On Foot," *Guardian Unlimited* (6 July 2006), http://www.guardian.co.uk/comment/story/0,,1813443,00.html (accessed July 15, 2006).

6... Jean Baudrillard, "The Spirit of Terrorism," trans. Rachel Bloul, http://cryptome.org/baud-terr.htm (accessed July 15, 2006).

7... See Paul Virilio, "Cold Panic," *Cultural Politics* 11 (2005): 27: "[A] third type of conflict, after 'civil war' and 'war between nations': namely, *war on civilians*; hence, also, the major political importance of the consequences of the (natural or industrial) *catastrophic accident* and the *massive attack* (whether anyone claims responsibility or not)" (emphasis in original).

Material Agency

Peter Testa and Devyn Weiser

The Emergent Design Group (EDG) develops theoretic frameworks and open-source software environments that integrate computational thinking with material processes. This trans-disciplinary approach incorporates and adapts the very latest programming techniques from artificial intelligence, artificial life, computational geometry, advanced structural engineering, and material science to establish a materially based methodology for generating architecture. These new methods of material computation engage ongoing developments in material science and advanced engineering in which materials are no longer fixed substances and morphogenesis supersedes morphodescription. EDG explicitly develops software tools that, like ALife, model component or material agency and distributed component interactions within complex structural and spatial systems. In each case EDG tools propose new control models—genetic, nonlinear, networked, and stochastic. These tools are original in focusing on agency and structure via material systems that articulate, embody, coordinate, and in some cases author actions or formal systems. This reliance on processes within materials reflects a phase beyond the mechanical era and a different version of systems thinking. Our work synthesizes both spatially and structurally oriented models of design and raises the promise of controlling growth through feedback and articulation within a whole developing structure. EDG's open-source software tools—including Agency: Architecture of Emergent Organizations (AgencyGP); Morphogenetic Surface Structures (MoSS); Generative Form Modeling (GENR8); and Weaver—study combinatorial spaces such as cell complexes, vector fields, combinatorial differential topology, and geometry.

Agency: Architecture of Emergent Organizations (AgencyGP)

AgencyGP, developed in the context of a research program with Herman Miller, Inc., in 2000, extends a genetic algorithm paradigm with the innovative use of user-programmable agent-based evaluation and analysis of evolving three-dimensional forms. It also serves as a test bed for interactive design–based evolutionary computation. Along with more conventional product and system design, we created an open-source software platform for generative modeling of emergent spatial organizations.

AgencyGP manifests our conviction that well-articulated design allows human and non-human actors to engage in novel compositions and reach new levels of

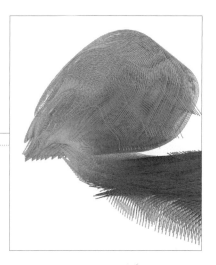

Weaver, Crochetscape

Agency GP, prototype office for Herman
Miller, Inc., generated using agent-based
genetic programming in Maya

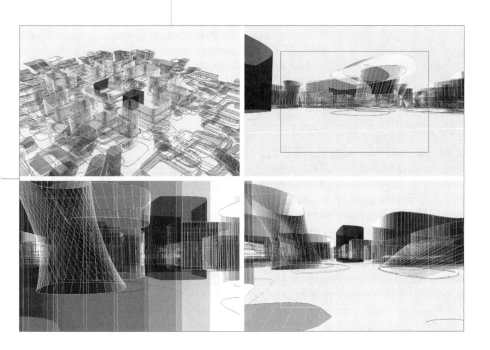

expressiveness and creativity. In this connectionist approach, novelty emerges from the tension of innumerable heterogeneous actors who negotiate their differences, expand their alliances, and continually redefine who they are and what they can do. From this perspective, AgencyGP is not a thing but networks that are the result of an ongoing series of negotiations between heterogeneous entities.

As in other EDG software systems, this design approach is implemented using Alias|Wavefront's Maya Package, a leading tool for the creation and visualization of complex virtual environments. Maya is widely used in the fields of three-dimensional animation for film and broadcast, but has only recently begun to be applied to explorations of morphology such as AgencyGP. Through Maya's API (Application Programming Interface) we build a genetic programming system operating over a language capable of expressing three-dimensional designs and the free-form deformation of space to generate populations of designs with agent-based evaluation. Maya's open architecture allows for software like AgencyGP to exploit the power of its inbuilt library of three-dimensional operations. When AgencyGP is invoked from within Maya, a C+ object is permanently attached to each NURBS (Nonuniform Rational B-Splines) curve. This C+ construct contains evolvable values pertaining to the shape and architectural function of the region the curve encloses. The object also contains an evolvable sequence of spatial transformations and Boolean operations in our GP language to be applied to this curve.

A significant innovation is that AgencyGP implements controls that allow the user to *interrupt*, *intervene*, and *resume* (IIR) the design-generation process under changing goal criteria. To our knowledge this is the first instance of direct user intervention in an evolutionary programming tool. In a departure from other tools, AgencyGP implements a set of operations to modify an external design that can be reverse mapped to the design's internal representation (that is, the representation manipulated by genetic operations). The internal language we have developed for evolution in the Genetic Programming (GP) system manipulates spatial constructs at the same level that a designer does when working in a three-dimensional modeling system. Therefore the individual commands of the language are meaningful to and useful by designers, ensuring the efficiency of IIR. Direct intervention in the design-generation process is significant in acknowledging the active and subjective role of the designer or groups of designers and users in setting variable and shifting criteria, including aesthetic preferences. In a departure from the optimization protocols underlying the use of Genetic Programming systems in the field of computer science, by implementing user intervention within AgencyGP we explicitly acknowledge that not all aspects of a design scenario or evaluative criteria can or need be coded into a software system. In this way AgencyGP is not conceived as a closed or synoptic system but open to creative manipulation and hacking of unprogrammed or unforeseen process sequences.

AgencyGP employs the determination of fitness from the point of view of various agents that inhabit the space. Agent-based fitness allows for a modular structure and the integration of multiple criteria for fitness. Agents may be humans or non-humans; they may also represent emergent organizational elements such as a group of users who express a coherent need, a resource that has allocation demands or a group of resources that provide a service; they may be structural parameters or codes of various derivation. Users can abstract the agent structure so that new agents may be developed and employed for new applications without rewriting the entire system. Virtually any criterion for evaluation can be coded and dropped in as an agent to our framework. The spatial effects of such an abstracted agent cannot be determined in any way other than to run the system under this agent's selective pressure. Since the descriptive language and representation of the individual designs is spatial, the system effectively translates non-spatial constraints into spatial hypotheses. This agent-based evaluation of fitness is well suited to expressing the conflicting, nonlinear, multi-level spatial requirements of emergent organizational structures.

In AgencyGP the designer specifies an initial condition. The state or condition of a complex system, over time, depends on its initial conditions. Dynamic non-deterministic systems that exhibit sensitive dependence on initial conditions are the main subjects of investigation in this type of emergent design process. From this beginning state the multi-tracked exploratory process of population evolution then provides a designer multiple avenues and alternative morphologies with which to interact at any point in time.

As a platform AgencyGP allows for new combinations of previously discrete systems and in so doing supports a critical, empirically based inquiry into the potentials but also limits of generative design tools. In time, users gain a first-hand understanding of the sensitive dependence of complex dynamic systems on initial conditions as well as the need within architectural investigations to continuously invent and recombine alternating digital and analog processes and sequences as opposed to series of steps that are all alike.

AgencyGP has been used for a wide range of design objectives by individual designers as well as major companies including Herman Miller and BMW North America, in form finding and generating complex 3D shaping environments. BMW employs AgencyGP in developing interactive scenarios between users, automobiles, and various urban and transportation environments. The potentials for this new type of software have only begun to be explored and have far-ranging applications in increasingly engineered natural and human-made contexts.

Morphogenetic Surface Structures (MoSS)

Where AgencyGP and other EDG projects such as the Java Toolbox interactively probe complex spatial organizations, Morphogenetic Surface Structures (MoSS) belongs to a stream of projects focused on structural morphology and generative engineering in the context of advances in material science and manufacturing.

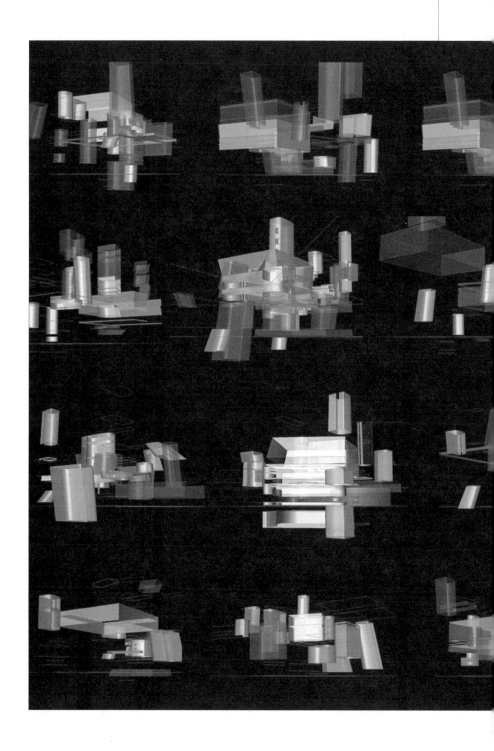

Agency GP, evolvable sequence of spatial
transformations and Boolean operations in
EDG's genetic programming language

Like AgencyGP, MoSS is written as a plug-in and seamlessly integrated into the Alias toolset. MoSS uses a specialized implementation of 3D Lindenmayer systems (L-systems) that grow surfaces in a 3D shaping environment by applying rewrite rules to an axiom with an accompanying interpretation of movement and drawing in space. In MoSS the designer specifies the grammar and guides surface growth by defining shaping forces and boundary conditions. The interface includes control factors that establish grammar, limit generation, and shape environment.

A significant feature of MoSS is that the environment dictates the final geometry of a surface or structure. The environment includes a user-defined volume (or bounding box) to force growth within its limits as well as different vectors of attraction that draw movement toward some forces and make others repulsive. This force vector is parameterized for the user to set, allowing for interaction with and control of the growth environment. Attractors and repellors (represented as plus and minus signs in the modeling environment) can be parameterized in terms of location and strength; they can be static or mobile and used to represent any number of forces within a structure or in the environment. Within MoSS it is also possible to generate multiple surfaces that mutually influence each other.

One example of a structural system developed within the MoSS research program is the Free-Form Honeycomb Truss. In this system, vertices of generated surfaces are joined to form an adaptive three-dimensional cellular structure or membrane. Using advanced composite materials, cell geometry, size, wall thickness, and depth may be continuously varied in response to nonlinear patterns of stress. This capacity for variability and interaction at all scales of a structure demonstrates how MoSS supports the development of new material forms that are co-evolved rather than assembled in a conventional sense.

As a structural system, MoSS is best understood as a network of adjacencies constituted as the result of interactions and combinations of forces. Each cell has a series of local stiffness to be considered, and the array of stiffness can be assembled into one large matrix. In this way we formulate a system in which substance and pattern are related and begin to move from atomistic (discrete) systems to finite deformation continuum mechanics models tied to non-isotropic materials and non-isotropic fields.

Generative Form Modeling and Manufacturing (GENR8)

To create a bridge between local and global simulation of cellular structures, in 2000 EDG began to implement GENR8, a software system that uses map L-systems. Map L-systems extend the expressive power of L-systems beyond branching structures to graphs with cycles called maps that represent cellular layers. GENR8 is a map L-system with geometric interpretation that operates by first establishing the neighborhood relations between cells, then assigning geometric parameters to the resulting

MoSS, L-system-based surface structure evolved within a 3D shaping environment

GENR8, instantiation of evolutionary algorithm-based surface grammar within a 3D shaping environment

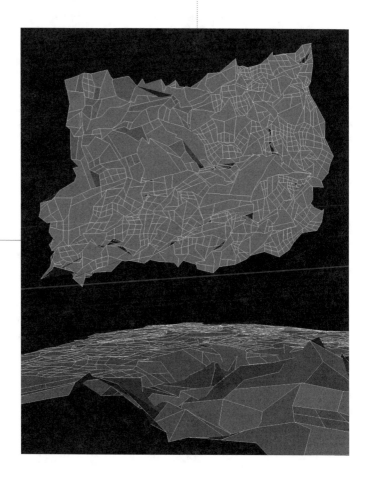

graph. Grammar-based rules specify a model's topology, which sequentially determines its geometry.

GENR8 is designed to accommodate iterative control exchange as it supports users introducing new formats and modifying process sequences including the ability to interrupt, intervene, and then resume an Evolutionary Algorithm (EA) tool. For example, five independent parameters or fitness criteria are implemented: size, smoothness, soft boundaries, subdivision, and symmetry. The different (independent) parameters can be used to express multilevel, nonlinear, and possibly conflicting design criteria. Similarly, the weight and parameters of any criterion can be changed at any time during a run. The user can also indirectly affect fitness by changing an individual element and inserting those copies into the population. It is also possible to insert another population (previously saved in a file) into the existing population.

A significant innovation in GENR8 is grammatical evolution that allows for a whole range of hybrid grammars. For example multiple surface grammars might interact within a user-controlled shaping environment and under user-set fitness criteria. These characteristics become increasingly relevant in the context of designed and non-isotropic materials. EDG's conceptual thinking is manifest in GENR8's capability to instantiate growth models with the potential to combine the atomic structure and mechanical properties of materials, and the macro behavior of the surface structure as a whole operating in a dynamic shaping environment. In this way tunable factors in the materials themselves may be adapted through mutualist feedback with the emergent structural morphology as a whole. The advantages of such a complex quasi-autonomous material system are significant as matter is effectively channeled to areas where it is needed and away from areas where it is not. The overall morphology is an open system that can theoretically be infinitely varied based on intrinsic and extrinsic conditions in which it operates.

Weaver
....

EDG's most recently developed tool, Weaver, is inspired by computer-controlled weaving and braiding. This application begins from the propensity of fiber-based composite materials such as carbon fiber to create complex tangled structures and the fabrication technology of pultrusion and filament winding. Using these techniques, woven and non-woven fibers can be formed into heterogeneous structural elements continuously varying in strength and other properties. The goal is to work with these material capacities and performances with diverse kinds of agency.

With EDG's Weaver, instead of surfaces the user creates threads and tangles. Weaver uses a grammar capable of describing and generating woven strands to a user-defined surface. The resulting weaves can be complex, and depend on both the description of the weave pattern and the topology of any user-defined surface or scaffolding in Maya on which Weaver is applied.

Weaver, Crochetscape

Weaver allows the user to specify custom weaves made up of any number of strands, with any cross section. While made of weak and light elements, the system is inherently resistant to severe stress since the structure can quickly distribute and therefore absorb forces through the entire web. In each case we approach the structure as a weak system that builds strength through networks by carefully intertwining weak elements, bands, or systems. A key characteristic of this structural morphology is that patterning, form, and organization are an informal or emergent effect. In contrast to structural differentiations characteristic of modernity, Weaver creates transversal connections, de-differentiations, linkages, and networks that challenge narrow optimization and specialization. As a software system Weaver supports a new class of structures understood as networks constituted as the result of interactions and combinations of forces.

In a significant departure from conventional architectural design, Weaver breaks down the distinction between representation and fabrication to establish continuity from drawing through manufacture and construction of the finished project. As demonstrated in our recent work, including the robotically pultruded Carbon Tower (2003), developed with ARUP, and Strand Tower (2006), toolsets such as Weaver are fundamental to creating new design environments with the capacity to reboot the construction industry—integrating design, engineering, material science, fabrication, logistics, and construction management.

Conclusion: Materialist Agential Combinatorics

Tools and techniques like AgencyGP, MoSS, GENR8, and Weaver enable new ways of thinking about the flow of control information and material agency in the shaping of space and structural morphology. This idea of becoming and change is one of the central methodological ideals of EDG. Our tools approach these issues experimentally, and in a range of ways shift away from form as something given to the outcome of a range of material processes in time. EDG's architectural research program is increasingly grounded in a materialist agential combinatorics as a means of framing contemporary forms of material agency and tying heterogeneous elements together in novel ways—a new calculus in which matter, pattern, and structural morphology search for each other through mutualist feedback. In this process, the inherent morphogenetic potential and continuously variable behavior of non-isotropic materials and structures is allied to organic computing. Rather than use overwhelming force, in each case we develop weak systems made up of cells, webs, and tangles that form informal, massively distributed structural networks. These new forms of material agency provide a platform for architecture within the context of the ongoing materials revolution.

Acknowledgments

....

The authors would like to thank Ian Ferguson, Simon Greenwold, Martin Hemberg, Markus Kangas, Axel Killian, and Una-May O'Reilly (co-director) of EDG and Emily White for original software development and implementation.

Selected Software

....

AgencyGP (2000)
Plug-in for Alias|Wavefront Maya
Principal Investigators: Peter Testa, Devyn Weiser, Una-May O'Reilly
Software Design: Simon Greenwold
http://mit.edu/edgsrc/www/agency/index.html

MoSS (1998-99)
Plug-in for Alias|Wavefront Studio
Principal Investigators: Peter Testa, Devyn Weiser, Una-May O'Reilly
Software Design: Markus Kangas
Research Assistant: Axel Killian
http://mit.edu/edgsrc/www/moss/index.html

GENR8 (2001-present)
Plug-in for Alias|Wavefront Maya
Principal Investigators: Una-May O'Reilly, Peter Testa
Software Design: Martin Hemberg
http://mit.edu/edgsrc/www/genr8/index.html

Weaver (2001-present)
MEL Script for Alias|Wavefront Maya
Principal Investigators: Peter Testa, Devyn Weiser
Software Design: Simon Greenwold
http://mit.edu/edgsrc/www/weaver/index.html

The Dom-in[f]o House

Dagmar Richter

DR_D (Design, Research, Development) was established in three different parts of the world with the aim of rethinking architectural design methods in the wake of the digital revolution. The DR_D Studio, in Los Angeles, uses international idea competitions to experiment with design processes, while the DR_D Office, in Berlin, applies these new processes to construction projects. The DR_D Lab—first established at UCLA, then relocated to the Art Academy in Stuttgart from 2002 to 2005, and back again to UCLA in 2006—is a research studio with graduate students working to produce experimental research-oriented projects for exhibition or publication purposes. All three organizations investigate common operations in design processes, keeping a critical attitude toward our political and cultural ideologies embedded in the process.

Inspired by Gottfried Semper's encouragement for the "adventure of research," DR_D has repeatedly taken up his well-known theory of cladding, as articulated in his 1851 essay "Textiles": "Scaffolds that served to hold, secure, or support [a] spatial enclosure had nothing directly to do with *space* or the *division of space*. They were foreign to the original architectural idea and were never form-determining elements to start with."[1] Semper's theories have lately enjoyed a revitalization through the introduction of digital design methods, which DR_D has put to use in its own design research experiments. Through the use of novel digital visualization instruments, the process of architectural design has undergone a principal reorientation. The deeply ingrained method of revealing, demonstrating, and making visible the constructive logic of a building has changed toward new methods of producing, with the help of film animation programs, principal surface effects. These new surfaces are considered to be capable of carrying their constructive properties as well as providing exceedingly embedded ornamental effects. In our research at the DR_D Lab, the designers were more interested in the notion of "special effects" than in the revelation of constructive processes based on an arts and crafts–defined process. This crafts-oriented constructive process, however, has vanished in order to give way to highly specialized and computerized construction processes. At stake for us was the question of how to define and deal with ornament in a post–digital revolution discipline.

In 1946 Albert Einstein wrote to Le Corbusier on the Modulor, calling it "a system of measurements which will make the bad difficult and the good easy."[2] Einstein's remark showed very clearly that the modern era was committed to an architect that used

 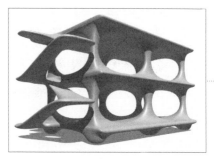

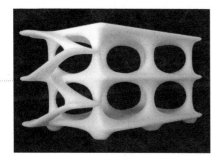 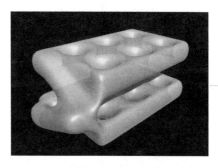

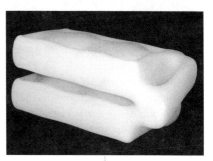

First Steps:

First translation as surface of
constructive skeleton

3D print of first translation

Second translation as surface of given
space

3D print of second translation

sophisticated systems in order to place assemblages of repetitive and mass-produced single elements within building systems. One of course could not have envisioned a method where new computer programs were able to process smooth geometries and manipulate surfaces that were simultaneously constructive and ornamental as a continuous non-assembled matter. Today, at least if one listens to the opinions of more mature colleagues, these programs are considered aesthetically challenging, as one risks reversing Einstein's promise—allowing those programs to make the bad easy and fast and good difficult.

Upon its move to Stuttgart in 2002, the DR_D Lab started to investigate the discipline's principal new methods of architectural design through the use of animation programs, using Le Corbusier's Domino House proposal as a jumping-off point. We chose this project for many reasons: first, it was and is handled as an all-encompassing icon for the modernist movement in architecture; second, the Domino House stood after World War I as the ultimate method for mass-produced housing; and third, this oft-published icon showed a clear disjunction between structure, interior surfaces, and decoration via furniture, where many performative aspects of the modern domestic were provided by additional items placed upon the structure. With the project Dom-in(f)o House, students were invited to join us at the Stuttgart Lab to research and produce an experimental research project that would instead integrate all domestic performative aspects into its computer-modeled surface.

Equipped with Semper's argument for the textile origin of architecture, we took on Le Corbusier's different texts and proposals from nearly one hundred years ago as highly contradictory instructions on how to handle structure and ornament in architecture.[3] As a kind of pedagogical exercise, Le Corbusier tried to teach the young and unformed architect about the principal elements of architectural building. As we studied the different translations of *Vers une architecture* from French into both English and German, it became apparent that the different wordings of Le Corbusier's categories showed our discipline's apparent difficulties in understanding the implications of this modern paradigm shift. The first category of greatest importance to Le Corbusier was *le volume*, translated into English as "mass," while in German became *Baukörper*, or "the building's body." This "body," in its importance and heaviness, was to be designed and defined, according to Le Corbusier's idealization, by the engineer, who was so much better equipped to assemble "according to universal rules" this "body" of the building. The second reminder of the universal principles of architecture was *la surface*, translated into German as *Aussenhaut*, or "the outer skin," though read in English as "surface." This surface or skin wrapped the building and gave it life—though according to Le Corbusier, this surface became "dangerous" for the young architect. He saw this surface as capable of acting as a parasite, a devourer of all good intentions, sucking up all architectural sophistication; therefore it was to be suppressed and controlled by the architect with rigor. *Le plan* in French, a "plan" (in English) was supposed to control this parasite, though in German it was no plan but a deliberate mark on the ground by the architect

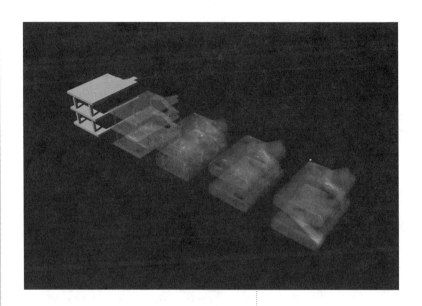

Development of prototypes:

Development from first translation to first horizontal surface prototype

Command: Integrate stairs and columns into the surface model

Result: Gleimbottle principle

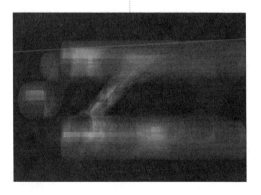

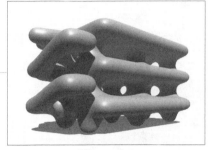
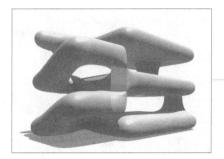

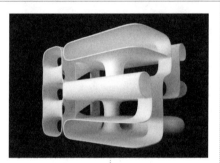

Development of first translation:

Command: equalize values

Command: equalize stair and platform values

Command: Loft closed surfaces through minimal surfaces in opposite directions

3D print of open model for stacking

3D print of closed model for horizontal attachment

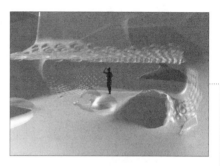

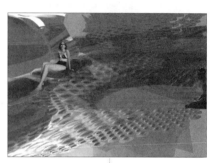

Application 1: Horizontal on water:

Attach centralized

Attach linear

Perspective of horizontal attachment

Perspective of underwater interior

Perspective of above-water exterior

(*Grundriss*). According to Le Corbusier, we could first detect structural contradictions that supported Semper's theory of cladding, followed immediately by a denial of this origin. Semper's words inspired many generations of modernists without questioning structurally its serious implications. He insisted on a surface effect as architecture's principal origin; Le Corbusier in contrast insisted on the visible structure, correctly placed by the unsentimental engineer, as the principal origin for architecture's expression and reading. Le Corbusier categorically contradicted the possibility of a principal surface effect of architecture as he vehemently tried to give the substance of architecture to the mass, body, and weight of its construction, belittling any tradition of ornamentation. At the same time, however, he recommended constructing his buildings such that only the surface as the vessel and form for the wet concrete shall be brought to the building site. Using local concrete ingredients could save weight and transportation costs, he wrote, thus having unconsciously incorporated Semper's view of the surface being architecture's main ingredient.[4]

The call for authenticity and truthfulness, which was to be demonstrated in the correct and readable construction and visible assemblage of the different building parts, was the basis of the modernists' concept of architecture. Today it has moved toward a surface effect, a moment, an affect the highly distracted user is at best teased by. This re-reflects Semper's own redefinition of architecture's origin, which has been followed by so many generations with different vigor. Attacks such as Loos's motto of ornament as crime or outcries over Louis Sullivan's decadent homosexual tendencies stayed with the discipline throughout the twentieth century as the expression of our suppressed subconscious since Semper found the ornament to come straight from our ancient cultures' most basic expressions. Those repeated attacks never ended after Semper's shake-up, and he himself was confronted with plenty of hostility after his text was published. The question of how to define and deal with ornament, and with this of architecture's inherent femininity, is an issue that reveals the subconscious of the discipline through permanent seepages and resulting suppression. The traditional architect then countered with condescension toward the ornament as the expression of a primitive and unworthy cultural enterprise. Semper's own findings of the architectural surface to be the mother of all things stayed with us in Stuttgart and at UCLA as a constant guiding light along our explorations.

As a test object, we therefore used Le Corbusier's Domino House as a means of comparing Semper's theories of cladding with the principal logic of Le Corbusier's design process in relationship with his vehemently described principal categories for how architecture should be defined. We wanted to learn more about these principals and how they could be theorized and applied today in a computer-driven design process. We started to work under the hypothesis that today the discipline's principal definitions and concepts of materiality as its inner core have moved away from the modern definition of architecture's authentic heavy and substantial materiality, and toward a primary modeling of surface effects through filmic animation programs.

Application 2: Horizontal as low-density
housing:

Perspective of horizontal attachment-north

Perspective of horizontal attachment-south

Site plan inserted at Weissenhof Stuttgart

Application 3: Vertical stacking as
high-density housing:

Perspective of vertical model

opposite:
samples of surface library built up by the
students

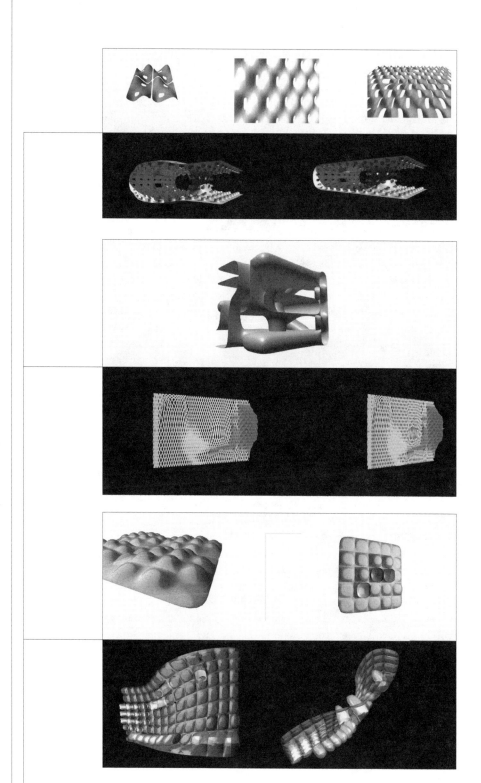

We directly investigated the old and then produced the new, non-standard "Dom-in(f)o" skeleton in 2002–03, with its indefinite variables, dependent on the performance criteria used as parameters. In this project, performance criteria as connection, non-hierarchical relationships, communication, adaptability, and surface-as-structure were directly linked to the transformations from the old to the proposed new surfaces. Instead of originally attaching all additional performances after the fact to the mass-produced skeleton that performs only one task—to be erect—we used our performance criteria to entirely drive the transformative process of the given surface by the original. This means that the skeleton was permanently challenged with then-new criteria including atmosphere, humidity, temperature, light, recycling, supply, and waste. In the first phase of this research project we arrived at the stage at which the original skeleton and its cladding became one. This skeleton then underwent a second test phase in fragments, where additional aspects of atmosphere and visual traits were used as transformative forces.

The research unit of the DR_D Lab at the Art Academy Stuttgart has produced several investigations reaching from an analysis of the existing icon and how it is automatically read through surface animation programs to many new readings of the resulting prototypes at hand. We used contemporary social data and its new demands to create new housing models for different speeds and velocities for our prototypes. We came up with a collection of skeletal prototypes, which directly test and link the theoretical discussions to a new topology for living.

Two distinct conditions are shown. First, the "skeleton" of the Dom-in(f)o House, in which a direct link to the new role of the architectural surface as a performing surface is made through a prototype with new combinations of structure and surface, inside and outside, mass production and adaptability. Second, the Dom-in(f)o House's "veneer" and adaptable "furnishing" is shown, where the further development of the house is demonstrated through the extensive use of our new surface library. All members of the DR_D Lab initially built up our surface library by testing different performance criteria as visual access, filtering, shading, body support, and ability to contain and use water within a 10-by-10-meter surface.

After the found prototype was remodeled through an animation program into the required surface construction, the new skeleton was permanently bombarded with performance requirements over time. First, the possibility of high-rise stacking for both short-term and long-term living was tested through abstract scenarios in metropolitan global areas. A dense urban public space connected all units through the vertical urbanscapes. Second, the possibility of low-rise through single attached units in a suburban-type setting was tested for short-term and long-term living. Here we tried to develop a new possibility for connecting the surrounding landscape to the different units as well as the possibility to interconnect and interweave water outside and inside, and one's neighbor with each other. All models then tried to describe a novel form of topography for living in our time.

DR_D Lab

Principal: **Prof. Dagmar Richter**
Research Director: **Jonas Luther**
Research Assistants: **Dina Krunic, Martijn Eefting, Erik Hökby**
Members of the Lab: **Daniela Boog, Ines Klemm, Klaudius Kegel, Claudia Kreis, Johannes Pellkofer, Philipp Rehm, Michael Scheuerer, Tomoko Oki, Isabell Ziegler**

Notes

....

1...Gottfried Semper, "Textiles," in *Style in the Technical and Tectonic Arts; or, Practical Aesthetics* (Los Angeles: The Getty Research Institute Publications, 2004), 248.

2...Willy Boesiger, *Le Corbusier* (Basel: Birkhauser, 1998), 86.

3...See the different translations of Le Corbusier's *Vers une architecture* (Paris: Collection de "L'Esprit Nouveau," Editions Artraud, 1923), 11, 21, and 31; in German, *Ausblick auf eine Architektur*, ed. Ulrich Conrads and Peter Neitzke, trans. Gärtner Hildebrandt, (Basel: Birkhäuser, 2001); and in English, *Towards a New Architecture*, trans. Frederik Etchells (New York: Holt, Rinehart and Winston, 1960), 25, 35, and 43.

4...See different descriptions by Le Corbusier in Chapter IV, in *Towards a New Architecture* on mass production, where he proposes to create a 7mm shell to be used as a form for cast concrete on site as if "filling into bottles"—see English version, pages 215–16.

From Data to Its Organizing Structure

....

George Legrady

Data as Cultural Information

....

My artistic research and projects during the past thirty years have steadily addressed the ways that information creation, collection, and processing through technological media such as the camera and the computer inherently influence and mediate the content that passes through them. Beginning with investigations about the properties of the photographic medium to current interests in data processing and its multilinear expression through interactive mixed realities installations, my practice has addressed algorithmic investigations for both image and data processing, the analysis and design of multilinear narrative form, and the role of metaphor in digital media representation, integrating motion sensing as a way to investigate the potential of the active participant as an influential component of the multimedia interactive event. My contribution to the field, since the early stages of the digital media arts' formation into a discipline, has been in intersecting cultural content with advanced data processing as a means of creating new forms of narrative experiences, expressed through data collection, data processing methodologies, and data visualization.

The projects to be described here have as common elements the procedures by which data becomes cultural information. The initial step is the recognition that data organization is a process by which to create meaning. This is followed by the search for, collection, and organization of data, which then must be described according to a system of rules, today labeled as "metadata," which is data about data, for instance a library catalog card that describes a book. In the sequence of the art projects presented here chronologically, the selection of data moves from the artist's choices to that of the spectator, meanwhile the artistic "voice" shifts from the data to its organizing structure. The projects also include a transition from "hardwired" relationships where the data relationships are predefined, to that of the implementation of a relational database, where the data exist separate from their structure and are then organized according to the search and retrieval based on their metadata. Most recent projects, such as the *Pockets Full of Memories*, use a self-organizing algorithm (SOA) to dynamically organize the data. These kinds of algorithms are also known

Catalogue of Found Objects, 1975
A vacant San Francisco lot was sampled
like an archaeological excavation site,
resulting in a collection of cast-off
objects to represent that location.
The artifacts were then classified and
catalogued against the same backdrop using
juxtapositions and repetition to reveal
similarities and differences.

as unsupervised learning algorithms as they iteratively achieve results that may not be initially defined at the start of the organizing process. They are also referred to as artificial neural networks, as they digitally model procedural properties of biological neural networks, such as activating rapid connections between all nodes in a system to see which ones have the highest compatibilities.

The organization and processing of data need to be communicated in some meaningful way following standards and conventions that have been learned through use and experience (think of the ATM, or library holdings). In the case of works of art that engage such technological processes, the spectacle nature of public museum exhibitions demands that the data and its organization processes become visible and staged to engage a public that expects to have an aesthetic experience and understand what they are witnessing within a limited time and based on common knowledge. The aesthetic expression is made meaningful for the public through narrative and choreography strategies through the audiovisual display of the information.

These fundamental aspects of digital media artworks have a legacy in the mid-1960s minimalism and conceptual art movements.[1] Conceptual art distanced itself from material expression by shifting emphases to systems, processes, and structures, where the artist's organizational method became the means and focus of artistic expression as a way to emphasize the cognitive, intellectual aspect of the art process. The Fluxus movement of the same period also pronounced its commitment to bypass commodity and institutional values by focusing on the insignificant, the unpretentious, on using mass-produced objects readily obtainable by anyone. A particular artistic project of interest from this period is the *Anecdoted Topography of Chance* by the Fluxus artist Daniel Spoerri, whose rich and complex artwork suggests parallels to Ted Nelson's invention of the hypertext. Spoerri heuristically cataloged and mapped a chance collection of found items, the chaos left behind on his kitchen table following a night of partying. He implemented a system of classification that today is familiar to those working with databases. Each object on the table was tagged by an ID number, visually coded on a two-dimensional map of the table, classified alphabetically, then described one item per page, followed by references and anecdotes, and cross-referenced by the translator and the editor who added their own commentaries, in essence producing in the early 1960s a multilinear database artwork where common everyday objects triggered rich literary comments, personal narratives, and associative linkages.

Catalogue of Found Objects

A photographic work, *Catalogue of Found Objects*, produced while I was a graduate student at the San Francisco Art Institute some thirty years ago, embodies many of the research questions my current digital projects investigate about how cultural meaning, aesthetic resonance, and artistic expression result through the organization of information.[2]

In 1975 I stood at a vacant lot, contemplating photographing the visually intriguing texture of disorganized detritus, weeds, discarded objects, and general chaos representative of such transitional spaces that accumulate a history of their own through the build-up of junk randomly contributed by passersby. Imagining myself to be an archeologist in some future situation, I began to study the range of objects and collected a sampling of them that were of varying degrees of cultural interest, portable, and could be considered representative of the consumer culture from which they came. The transition from found samples to cultural document and artistic expression occurred through the process of classification and cataloging by systematically photographing the objects against a common backdrop to give the impression of classified data, conveyed by the backdrop's resemblance to computer printout paper. The formal structure of the artwork evolved as a consequence of using photography as a classification medium, which necessitated sub-unit groupings based on thematic relationships, sequences, and narrative flow. The resulting two-dimensional grid structure of images consisted of six vertical columns, each holding six images, for a total of thirty-six equal-sized panels that visualized the sampled objects like a statistically analyzed computer printout. The narrative flow began at the upper far–left column moving downward, then to each column of images eventually terminating at the far right–bottom image. Each vertical strip of six images functioned aesthetically as individual units, with each panel aesthetically linked to what was above or below it. The visual organization of objects in the columns guided the eye for a vertical viewing.

My classification methodologies relied on aesthetic, syntactic, and cultural decisions. I proceeded to cluster the objects and sequence their groupings according to what made sense in terms of the interrelations of the objects within the range of the sum of all the elements. A system and lexicon came into being, resulting in an ordered state from the initial set of unrelated data. My approach reflected what the anthropologist Claude Lévi-Strauss described in the opening chapter of his book *The Savage Mind*, that "any classification is superior to chaos and even a classification at the level of sensible properties is a step toward rational ordering....The decision that everything must be taken account of facilitates the creation of a 'memory bank.'"[3] Even though an order was achieved through the relations based on the objects' properties, the overall impression of the work is a consequence of an orchestration based on aesthetics. Two divergent modes of ordering were superimposed one on top of each other—one based on the literal properties of formal structure, the other based on aesthetic, poetic qualities of the featured objects. These guide the viewing experience not unlike studying a film one frame at a time, where each image is a sequence to the next. Through this viewing process, a narrative evolves as one assembles the subject matter considering the play of relations. This assembling has a cultural basis in the signifying semiotic and linguistic aspects of cultural objects as data and the analysis of the context by which the data is situated. Today, these objects would be evaluated in a more precise manner, initially labeled according to their measurable metadata properties such as function, material, color, scale, and then followed by aesthetic and associative values depending on what the intended goal may be.

The collection and processing of data have been an intrinsic part of cultural knowledge-making since the dawn of history, and this has exponentially increased through mass-scale digitization. Databases are now one of the most dominant features of how we organize our society, from credit-card records to supermarket transactions to statistics and academic and scientific research. We now invest extensively in data mining as a means to uncover unsuspected relationships and to summarize the data in novel ways that are both understandable and useful.

An Anecdoted Archive from the Cold War

The _Anecdoted Archive from the Cold War_ produced in 1992, was my first digitally based multimedia artwork to explore the potential of nonlinear narrative form.[4] The project was unique in its time as it brought together cultural and aesthetic methodologies from the disciplines of fine arts photography, conceptual art, and humanities visual culture with the new technological developments that at the time were primarily featured in commercially driven marketing media fairs. The project addressed the specific condition of late-twentieth-century cultural hybridity resulting out of geographical and political migration in the age of global corporate mass-media cultivation. The intent of the project was to create a narrative-driven information environment consisting of cultural odds and ends that somehow provided a fragmented overview representing my autobiographical history from a number of socio-political, geographical cultural worlds during the Cold War era. The cultural information consisted of a collection of digitized personal and official documents, objects, sounds, films, etc. in my collection at the time the Berlin Wall came down. The objects were gathered over time as relics and mementos, but also as research material focused on the lexical and syntactic nature of Socialist iconography that I had studied in the mid 1980s. The range of objects is quite varied: CIA documents, children's propaganda books, a carved Soviet anti-aircraft shell, personal family letters and photos, videos of family life, footage of monuments. I chose the contested term "archive" in the title to infuse the authoritative meaning generated by that word onto the body of disparate personal and public material housed and stored side-by-side in my digitally constructed database. The collection of digitized images, cinematic samples, sounds, texts, and documents, consisting of over sixty stories and objects, were published as an interactive CD-ROM at a time when this medium proposed innovative possibilities. Since then, the medium has been displaced by the internet.

The data was thematically organized into eight sections and given form using a visual menu consisting of the architectural floorplan of an authoritative institutional

An Anecdoted Archive from the Cold War, 1993

An interactive installation and CD-ROM publication that explores the archive as a multilinear narrative. Over sixty stories and objects of personal and official documents from Stalinist Hungary of the 1950s in the artist's possession are classified into eight chapters and visually organized according to the floor plan of the former Hungarian Communist propaganda museum.

Top left: Floor plan
Top right: Lunar exploration
Bottom left: Kiss on the bridge, now and then
Bottom right: Propaganda posters

Slippery Traces, 1995
250 postcards are organized into
twenty-four chapters with each image
interconnected to others through a
database, using subsections in each image
as metadata. The interactive installation
and CD-ROM addresses twentieth-century
cultural representation in the form of a
multilinear narrative in which images are
linked to each other according to literal,
metaphorical, and associative properties.
Top left: Installation space
Top center: Jumping for ball
Top right: Native American dance
Bottom left: Beach scene
Bottom center: "The Big Jump," all images
Bottom right: Chinese opera dance

structure, the former Hungarian Socialist propaganda museum. Superimposing classified groupings of personal materials and narratives onto such a metaphoric floor plan provided structural cohesiveness and a rich narrative potential where political data and the contrast of the public and the private become recontextualized. As with the *Found Objects* project, the challenge lay in defining a method by which to categorize, catalog, and classify the range of objects in such a way that cohesiveness could be achieved. The architectural floorplan became the means to categorize the data into sub-sections or chapters represented by rooms. Through the process of viewing the various objects and their stories in a sequence determined by their choices, each spectator would assemble a specific narrative determined by the sequence that may be different from another's.

As the majority of the objects and stories in the *Anecdoted Archive* were related to others classified in the eight sections, this project opened the way to consider relational databases as a potential authoring medium for artistic and literary narrative development. Given that a story might be considered as an assemblage of a set of data (objects, sounds, texts, documents, etc.) organized within a particular structure, the potential sequence could be evaluated computationally by analyzing each data's attributes.

Slippery Traces

The *Slippery Traces* project (1996) was the direct result of implementing the database as an organizing and navigational structure within which each data was relationally linked to others defined by rule-sets.[5] The database contains approximately 240 commercially made postcards which were selected based on subject matter, interesting compositions, socio-political significance, and oddities that made visible the main themes of twentieth-century global representations. A number of personally relevant images were also included. Among the images can be found family portraits from the 1920s to 1940s printed on postcards, places I have been, and cultures that shaped me in various ways. I was searching for images that were interesting in their content and structure, images that were culturally significant, or relevant subject matter or visually intriguing compositions that express a perception based on the photographic paradigm. For instance, images of conventionality and banality such as tourist sites, business arrangements, advertising; images of the social order representing work, industry, military, family; images that make visible the technical in the photographic, such as being blurred or oddly framed; personal images, images that expressed the passing of time; images of transgression, articulating colonialism, the exoticizing or eroticizing of the non-Western culture; images of abundance, images of the absurd stated through the exaggerated, the touristic, the play of similarity, the play between the natural and the cultural such as dressed-up animals; images of fear, such as assassination, Nazi group photos, fire, destruction; images that play on ethnocentrism, racism, or stereotypes such as a Gulf State Arab count-ing money; and images that expressed the poetic and the sublime.

The images were organized into twenty-four chapters with such titles as "Na-ture & Culture," "Morality Tales," and "Ancient Monuments." These emerged out of the clustering of the chosen images into groups. The navigation through the images was limited to viewing segments of one image at a time, and in the process the view-er would encounter "hot spot"–defined areas over parts of the image which, when clicked on, would then bring up another image from another chapter thematically linked to the clicked area's subject matter (for instance, clicking on a building in the image may bring up another postcard with architecture). The use of small vi-sual fragments within each postcard as the metadata allowed for complex sequences because of the polysemous nature of the images and their potential literal, meta-phoric, and associative relationships to other images.

Slippery Traces had its roots in a two-projector slide show created to explore the ways that the meanings of images change when juxtaposed with other images. Im-ages are normally seen in relation to each other, and like words positioned together in a sentence, they oscillate each other, slightly expanding, readjusting, impercep-tibly transforming their meaning through contrast, association, extension, differ-ence, etc. Transferred to the nonlinear dynamic environment of the computer, the shifts in meaning are exponentially increased as the images are freed from their slide-tray linear positions, to be constantly re-situated in relation to each other as determined by criteria defined in the computer code. The result is an imaginary three-dimensional, nerve cell–like membrane network in which all 240 images are interlinked with over 2,000 connections crisscrossing to form a unified whole. Con-nections, or hot spots, have something thematically in common with the image they call up. Each time the viewer clicks on a hot spot to move to another image, he or she weaves a path in this dense maze of connections.

The viewer steps from one information unit selected out of a range of possible choices to another, also selected out of other possible choices. These linkages are de-fined through keywords hidden from the viewer in the database according to common literal or metaphoric properties. The work's title, *Slippery Traces*, makes reference to the psychoanalyst Jacques Lacan's particular use of the term "slip" and slippage to describe the unstable relationship between a sign and its meaning.[6] Lacan noted that meaning emerges only through discourse—that is, that the meanings of things are defined not in themselves but through their relation to other signs. He argues against the Saussurian notion that there is a stable relation between a signifier and what it refers to. Consider Jacques Derrida's observation that in the construction of meaning, a signifier always signifies another signifier: no word is free from metaphoricity.[7] The example of the dictionary is offered. When we search for the meaning of a word, our recourse is to look in a dictionary where instead of finding meaning we are given other words against which to compare our word. From this we can gather that meaning, oth-erwise expressed as the term "signified," emerges through discourse, as a consequence of displacements along signifying chains. Both of these references consider meaning as taking place through the interaction of information modules sequenced in relation to each other. *Slippery Traces* evokes the cinematic montage sequence through the linear ordering of images chosen through hot spot links, but in contrast to the cinematic model, the narrative potential in this interactive work resides in the interplay of the viewer's choice, chance, and the encoded structure of the database.

Pockets Full of Memories

Whereas meaning is constructed in *Slippery Traces* through the build-up of a visual sequence according to the viewers' choices navigating within a multilayered database structure that embodies the artist's vision of the relationship of images and their associative significance, the *Pockets Full of Memories* project (2001–06) shifts emphasis to position the audience as the key content and meaning provider through their contribution of scanned objects and descriptions into a growing database.[8] The collection of cultural data is then continuously organized throughout the length of the exhibition by an algorithm that positions objects in relation to each other based on degrees of similarities and differences and then presents the results as a large projection featuring all objects that can fit on the screen. This spatially organized map can also be accessed on the internet, where comments can be added to any of the objects, further enhancing their cultural meaning.

Pockets Full of Memories is an interactive installation that involves a three-step process of data collection, data processing, and data visualization. Using a scanning station not unlike an ATM interface, the users digitally scan their objects, then describe them by filling out a touchscreen questionnaire with descriptive keywords, rating their properties, then providing demographic information. The data accumulates throughout the length of the exhibition. The Kohonen self-organizing map algorithm is used to organize the data on a continuous basis, moving the images of the objects into an ordered state according to similarities defined by the contributors' semantic descriptions. The archive of objects is projected large-scale on the walls of the gallery space showing various visualizations such as the objects positioned in the 2D matrix, their movement over time, and textual descriptions.

At the start of the exhibition, the database is empty, growing through the public's contributions. The algorithm organizes the data throughout the exhibition to arrive at a final ordered state at the end of the exhibition. The phenomenon of proceeding from small local actions (each contribution) to arrive at a final ordered state is called *emergence*, as the order is not determined beforehand but emerges over time through the local interactions generated by the algorithm each time a new object enters the database. In this sense, the system has been defined as self-organizing.

This project addresses the collection, organization, and presentation of data as a conceptual entity beginning with data as organizing system; data as expression

Pockets Full of Memories, 2001-2005
The museum public contributes to an
archive by digitizing an image of an
object in their possession. The sum of
the archive of objects is continuously
being organized by a Kohonen self-
organizing map algorithm, positioning
objects of similar descriptions near
each other. The archive of objects is
projected on a large gallery wall and
accessed on the internet.
1. Installation, Cornerhouse Gallery,
Manchester, UK
2. Questionnaire-object attributes
3. Questionnaire-demographic info

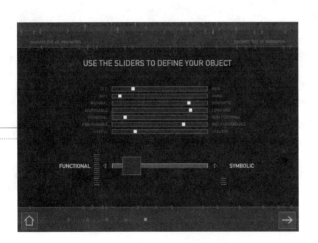

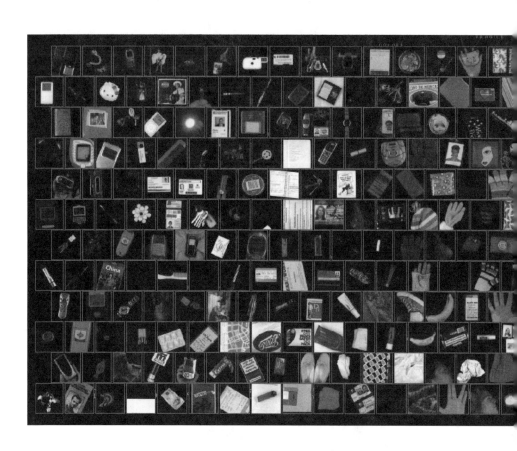

Pockets Full of Memories, 2001-2005
4. 2D map projection

through individual contribution; data as cultural artifact through digitizing, semantic description, and attribute rating; and data as processed information, classified, organized, and visualized in the exhibition space and the internet as an information-exchange meeting point with online commentary.

Making Visible the Invisible

Contemporary society's infrastructure is encoded in databases through our interactions in supermarkets, public transit systems, educational institutions, libraries, etc. Our collective behavior is collected, measured, and statistically evaluated to become the determining forces that reshape these information environments. *Making Visible the Invisible* (2004–05) is an artistic work that explores the informational infrastructure of the Seattle Public Library by statistically analyzing and then visually mapping the public's interactions with the library through the borrowing and return of library books, CDs, and DVDs.[9] In this way, one can potentially have a window into what may be "general concerns" or what the community may be "thinking" or considering as interesting information based on the actions of the library clients.

The project is a commission for the Seattle Public Library designed by the architect Rem Koolhaas, who has reformulated many conventional aspects of the library environment. The commission came about as a result of the library's interest in commissioning artworks from "artists whose work deals with social structures, people and systems"[10] to produce projects that "address in a thoughtful or analytical way, the dynamic systems, changing social and political climate, or underlying intellectual assumptions that characterize the library."[11] The finished project consists of custom-designed software that collects, analyzes, and filters data of clients' actions checking out books and media, with the results featured on six LCD screens horizontally positioned behind the main information librarian's desk in the large "Mixing Chamber" designated open space.[12]

Artistic commissions such as this one that engage complex cultural and engineering components must satisfy varying sets of interests. First, there is the public art commission component, which demands fulfillment of engaging the public through an aesthetically rewarding experience. This involves featuring choreographically designed active animations that achieve a balance between providing the aesthetic experience and also communicating meaningful information that goes beyond mere illustration. Information retrieval and visualization form the basis of the new information visualization discipline that has evolved out of the intersections of information library sciences and computer science. The intent with an artistic project like this one is to approach data analysis and its visualization in such a way that it provides new forms to experience the data, shaped by dramaturgic and choreographic methods of organization in space to achieve unexpected associative and metaphorical relations as a means to reveal new forms and patterns that will hopefully be able to communicate in a fuller and innovative way that which words and statistical information by themselves would not be able to.

Artistic practice has a long history of arriving at aesthetic resolution through the exploration of the plasticity of the material used in creating a work. In the case of custom software design, unexpected results are achieved through the interplay of an initial concept that is then transformed through experimentation to arrive at new and interesting outcomes. In this way, data processing as an art practice can be thought of as a time-intensive form of exploratory writing where the outcome is a consequence of the experimentation of how the syntax of mathematical models are applied and perturbed. But prior to the experimentation, standardized procedures have to be determined by which the incoming data is collected and organized over time, and this work requires careful planning and appropriate expertise; the *Making Visible the Invisible* commission involves complex engineering to collect and process the data in such a way that the system can function efficiently for the next ten years, the length of the commission. Rama Hoetzlein and Mark Zifchock have been the engineers responsible for the technical design of the organization, processing, and visualization of the incoming data, and the development of the Seattle project animations are an outcome of the back and forth conversations between artist and engineers.

Algorithmic Visualizations

Computer code development is an exciting and engaging medium, but in contrast to the visible presence of the physical, materially based artwork, software is a medium and material form that is hidden from view, and therefore outside of the reach of the spectator except through its eventual visual expression. My first encounters with the medium occurred in the mid-1980s with the first affordable digital image processing technologies becoming available through the AT&T Targa Vision system. The integration of computer programming with digitized images made it possible to bridge significantly different worlds such as fine arts photography, photographic visual culture theory and criticism, and the language and concept–based methodologies of the conceptual art of the 1960s. At that time it was revealing to experience the power of computer programming, a language-based instruction set system that activated processes at the click of the "enter/return" button and undid them with the "undo" button.

One of the most discussed topics in the field of photography and visual culture in the 1980s focused on the discrepancy between the apparent transparency of the optical-mechanical image and the cultural agenda. My first experimentations were therefore focused on how the technological computer apparatus could analyze, extract, filter, transform, and thereby lead to assumptions about the make-up of the photographic image, the dominant visual medium of the twentieth century that, even 150 years after its discovery, was still considered to be a transparent medium of

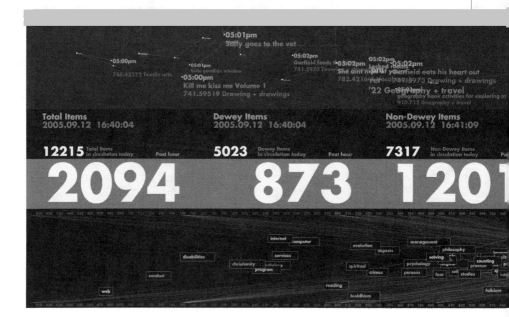

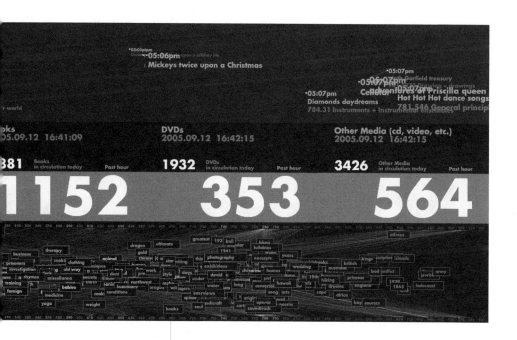

Making Visible the Invisible, 2004-2005
An installation of six plasma screens
behind the main librarian's desk in
the Mixing Chamber area of the library
features visualizations based on
statistical analyses of the circulation
of nonfiction books, CDs, and DVDs,
catalogued according to the Dewey Decimal
System, going in and out of the library's
collection.

representation. The transformation of the image into a stream of numbers further complicated the whole discourse of technological visual representation and the analysis focused on the function of the author's belief systems in creating the image.

My search in bridging computer-generated processes with fine arts photography at a time when artistic experimentation was limited to a small community who had access to resources and technologies, and production of digital images were not readily available, led me to surveillance and satellite image–processing computer code literature. This literature guided me to experimentations with explorations of mathematical processes related to noise and randomness, such as frequency modulations, 2D convolutions, adaptive algorithms, neural-net implementation, and pattern matching, leading to studies in image coherence, perception, and enhancing visual concepts about the new digital image.

These approaches had strong potential metaphorical values for conceptually exploring the relationship between images, syntax, language, and technological processes, in particular through the programming of randomness and visual noise, derived from discipline-specific interests at the time such as information theory, and fractal research related to chaos theory. I was particularly interested in the question of the veracity of the photographic image, when it became obvious that digital alterations in images could take place without noticeable traces.[13] The process of the artist writing computer code that generates an image raises interesting questions of authorship, complicating the question of where the artistic voice occurs—in the writing of the computer code or in the expression of the code when the image is generated. The initial experimentations were first presented on computer screens and then on Fujichrome inkjet prints in the late 1980s, when an early prototype system was made available in Los Angeles.

Algorithmic Visualizations (2003–present) is a generic term to describe a range of projects that are a continuation of a series of experimentations begun in the mid-1980s to produce images that were created purely through computer programming language. At some point in the process of investigating what could be possible through image-processing algorithms, it became obvious that by accentuating certain aspects of the algorithms, the process itself could generate visualizations without the need for an original referent photographic image to transform.[14] These resulted in abstractions that were pure expressions of the algorithm itself—for instance, in comparison to music, as if the noise to be filtered out from a song would become enhanced and replace the song itself.

Conclusion

All of these artistic research projects engage with cultural artifacts in search of an organizing system. The artifacts are identified, and their cultural values appraised, shifting to a search for linguistic, syntactic methodologies by which to define relationships,

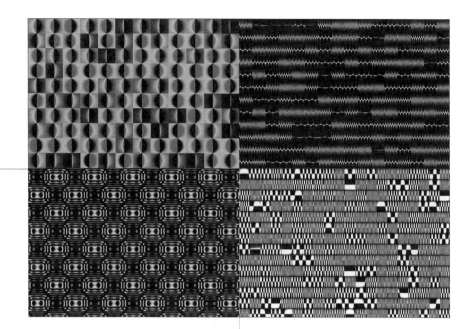

Algorithmic Visualizations, 2003-2005
"Algorithmic Visualizations" consists
of images created directly from
mathematical equations that have their
origins in image-processing algorithms
used to enhance or analyze digitized
images. This approach consists of rule-
based processes that integrate frequency
modulations, adaptive algorithms,
randomness, and noise.

Hand-Painted Traffic Instruction
Billboard, Shanghai, 1984

sequences, and hierarchies of meaning. With the integration of digitization into the process of assembling data and information, cultural artifacts become translated into numerically evaluated data and encoded with metadata as a way to describe them. As a result, the numerically described data can be classified through basic mathematical operations of addition and subtraction, and numeric comparisons. The next step has been a search for greater complexity, expressed through emergent and self-organizing algorithms that can express relationships between the data based on more complex, "unsupervised" ways, primarily possible as a result of the increased speed of computational calculations. *Algorithmic Visualization* diverges from this direction, as the process itself emerges fully as source, medium, aesthetic form, and visual expression, without any need for data and cultural artifact. The power in this approach, as we know today, is the innovative potential of mathematical processes to lead us forward in terms of conceptual, aesthetic, and design directions. The complexity of the organizing principle and the noise within the system become the cultural artifacts that emerge as the dominant cultural voice.

From the simple to the complex, these projects have traced the relationship between cultural data and their organization defined through their structure and the activated mathematical processes. On the larger scale, one can consider these artistic works as expressions of general trends in the changing cultural conditions of the Information Society. Information management is the defining form of culture today as it positions us as citizens in performing according to economic and political models defined through the statistical outcome of collected data. Is our relationship to the institutional structures more or less humanizing as a consequence of the new world information technological order and its transformative expressions in the economic political zones? This is a complex and broad question beyond the limits of this chapter, but it does poignantly surface as I write this sitting in an elegant Euro-American coffee chain in the heart of Shanghai, where I have wireless access that keeps me connected to my cultural world and obligations. I am totally surrounded by the wild paced expression of multinational corporate technoculture expressed through *Blade Runner*–style high-rises, electronic billboards, shopping, and nonstop traffic, whereas some <u>twenty years ago I walked these streets</u> passing through neighborhood communities with everyone out on the street surrounding each block's TV set.

My mission at the time was to photographically document ideological, aesthetic, and cultural expressions in public billboards to compare with studies about the construction of meaning in Western corporate annual reports and East European Soviet-style visual iconography. From what I superficially see with my limited exposure to the cultural environment through visits to Beijing and here, the transformation of the past twenty years, which parallels the integration of information technologies into society, has moved economic-cultural time forward in global cosmopolitan centers like this one by what seems like centuries, so that we all find ourselves communally exchanging our data within a mathematically processed, networked global structure.

Notes

....

1...Edward Shanken, "Art in the Information Age: Technology and Conceptual Art," *Leonardo* 35, no. 4 (2002): 433–38.

2...See http://www.mat.ucsb.edu/~g.legrady/gl-Web/ Projects/fo/found_obj.html (accessed Sept. 7, 2006).

3...Claude Lévi-Strauss, *The Savage Mind* (Chicago: University of Chicago Press, 1962), 15.

4...See http://www.mat.ucsb.edu/~g.legrady/gl-Web/Projects/anecdote/Anecdote.html (accessed Sept. 7, 2006).

5...*Slippery Traces* was produced as an interactive installation, first presented at the ISEA 95 exhibition in Montreal and subsequently in a number of museums, as well as in the traveling exhibition Deep Storage, curated by the Siemens Kultur Programm. It was published in its CD-ROM version the following year in Artintact 3, by ZKM, and most recently exhibited in the ZKM, Future Cinema exhibition, 2003, and the Database Imaginary traveling exhibition by the Banff Centre for the Arts, 2004–2005. See http://www.mat.ucsb.edu/~g.legrady/glWeb/Projects/slippery/Slippery.html (accessed Sept. 7, 2006).

6...Dylan Evans, *An Introductory Dictionary of Lacanian Psychoanalysis* (London: Routledge, 1996).

7...Sarup Madan, *An Introductory Guide to Post-Structuralism and PostModernism* (Atlanta: University of Georgia Press, 1988), 12.

8...See http://www.mat.ucsb.edu/~g.legrady/gl-Web/Projects/pfom2/pfom2.html (accessed Sept. 7, 2006).

9...See http://www.mat.ucsb.edu/~g.legrady/glWeb/Projects/spl/spl/index.php (accessed Sept. 7, 2006).

10...Call for Artists, The Library Unbound: The Seattle Public Library, Arts & Cultural Affairs, 2003. See http://www.publicartonline.org.uk/case/seattle/unbound.php (accessed Sept. 7, 2006).

11...Ibid.

12...Rama Hoetzlein, PhD student in the UCSB Media Arts & Technology doctoral program, has been responsible for the technical design of the software.

13...George Legrady, "Image, Language & Belief in Synthesis," in Simon Penny, ed., *Critical Issues in Electronic Media* (New York: NYU Press, 1994).

14...See http://www.mat.ucsb.edu/~g.legrady/glWeb/Projects/algo2/algo2.html (accessed Sept. 7, 2006).

Beyond Code

C. E. B. Reas

The Open Work

In 1962 a young Umberto Eco wrote *Opera Aperta* (later translated into English as *The Open Work*). He described the concept of a work of art defined as structural relationships between elements that can be modulated to make a series of distinct works. John Cage, Alexander Calder, and Yaacov Agam are examples of artists working in this manner contemporary to Eco's text. While all artworks are interpreted by the individual, he distinguished the interpretation involved in this approach to making art as fundamentally different from that of a musician playing from a score or a person looking at a painting. An open work presents a field of possibilities where the material form as well as the semantic content is open.

As an artist working in the medium of computer software, the codes I've been writing for the past five years extend this idea and explore the themes of instability and plurality. These works are continually in flux, perpetually changing the relationships between elements and never settling into stasis. Each moment in the performance of the work (by the artist or another individual) further explains its process, but the variations are never exhausted. The structure is not imposed or predefined, but through the continual exchange of information, unexpected visual form emerges. Through directly engaging the software and changing the logical environment in which it operates, new behavior is determined and additional channels of interpretation are opened.

This software is the basis for my explorations into print, animation, installation, and responsive works. I work in printed media to expose the density of my processes and to provide a precise image of the state of a system at one moment in time; I work in animation to precisely choreograph the development of the process; I create installations to explore the potential of relating my processes to the human body and architectural space; I build interfaces and objects that allow people to directly engage with the software to enable an understanding of the relation between the elements. It is through these different perspectives that a more complete understanding of the process emerges.

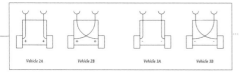

Valentino Braitenberg's Vehicles 2A, 2B, 3A, 3B. The semicircles represent sensors and are attached to the motors in different configurations.

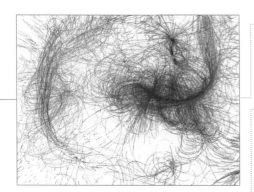

Tissue Software (2002) explores the movements of synthetic neural systems. People affect the software by positioning a group of points on the screen.

Tissue Type C-03, 2002

Tissue Type B-06, 2002

Tissue Type D-05, 2002

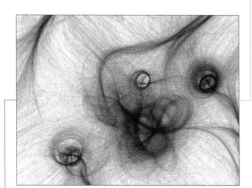

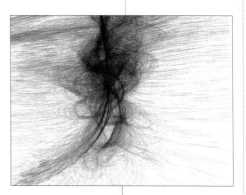

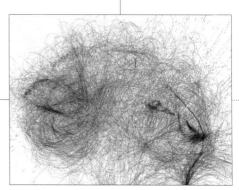

Perspectives on a Process
....

MicroImage is a series of software, prints, and animations developed from 2001 to 2003. The concept for *MicroImage* originated with the book *Vehicles: Experiments in Synthetic Psychology* by the neuroanatomist Valentino Braitenberg.[1] Braitenberg spent his career studying the nervous systems of insects and mammals, distilling generalizations about how nervous systems work. He wrote by researching "certain structures within animal brains that seemed to be interpretable as pieces of computing machinery because of their simplicity and/or regularity."[2] He uses the term *synthetic psychology* to define the construction of personality/behavior through building up structures of *computing machinery*, and defines a series of thirteen conceptual constructions, or vehicles, by gradually building more complex behavior with the addition of more machinery.

The software processes in *MicroImage* are analogous to Braitenberg's Vehicles 2 and 3. Simple layers of code combine to create the deceptively complicated behavior of these software machines. Each machine has two simulated sensors to detect the environment and two simulated actuators to propel itself. The relationships between the sensors and actuators determine the specific behavior for each machine. In the thousands of software machines simultaneously running, there are four distinct types, each specified with a color. The architecture of the machines are shown in the figure on page 167. The semicircles at the front (top) represent the sensors, and each rectangle at the bottom represents a motor. Each machine has a variable speed, direction, and position, but each shares the same size, turning rate, and maximum speed.

I first approached visualizing Braitenberg's machines through software. Transferring their behavior from diagrams to computer code required making many decisions about the precise distance between each sensor, the speed of each vehicle, and if there should be any perturbations on their simulated surface. After making preliminary studies, I decided to represent each vehicle as a thin graphic line connecting each vehicle's most recent locations (coordinates). Each segment of the line connects a previous location of the vehicle to a more recent location to visualize its speed and degrees of curvature. The motion of each vehicle type is controlled by changes to the simulated environment. People may affect the software by positioning the series of three points that define the environment. They experience an awkward sense of control as their actions have a direct but imprecise effect on the software. It is not possible to directly control the software machines, but their behavior can be encouraged and intuitively understood. Small changes in the positions of the stimuli create large global changes in the movements of the vehicles. If there are no stimuli, each vehicle moves in a straight line, but as each new point is added, the vehicles respond according to their simulated wiring. The software offers a near-infinite set of images, each dependent on the configuration of points that compose the environment.

Because the software implementation of *MicroImage* is continually in motion, it is impossible to look at the precise forms that emerge from the interactions between the vehicles and their environment. In addition, because the resolution of computer monitors is so low (72 pixels per inch), it is difficult to precisely see how the lines are positioned in space. I therefore began making static images from the *MicroImage* software to have a different perspective on the system. To make these images at a higher resolution than the default screen, I began exporting each line as a series of vector line segments, which allowed them to be printed at resolutions up to 2,880 dots per inch. Over time, I modified the software by changing the parameters of the vehicles' behavior, modifying the line length, and changing the number of vehicles. I challenged some of the assumptions in the original software by changing the way the sensors were related to the motors by testing a series of different nonlinear relations. Over time, five distinct software variations were produced to show a range of ways to interpret Braitenberg's original text. Through working with the software over a period of months, I exhausted the range of potential images produced through each software variation and made eight prints from each to show the potential variation in the system. Each print was made while working actively with the software by changing the environment and then exporting specific frames. Looking at these prints displayed on a wall gives a distinctly different view of the software than can be gleaned from working with the interactive version.

The type of images created with live software like *MicroImage* is limited by the amount of information a computer can process at thirty frames per second. To move beyond this restriction, I began exploring *MicroImage* through rendered animation. Because of the possibility to increase the time for calculating and drawing each frame, creating the animation allowed the numbers of vehicles displayed to increase from two thousand to five hundred thousand. This significantly changed the way the *MicroImage* process is perceived by the viewer, shifting the focus away from line and motion and placing the emphasis on mass and depth. The complexity of the environment was also increased so up to eight stimuli now interacted with the vehicles. Over the course of one month, I produced a twelve-minute animation.

Working on the animation led to the idea for a different software interpretation that would simulate the density of the animation. Rather than clearing the screen and redrawing each frame, I began accumulating each frame on top of the previous, allowing the visual data to continually build over time, thus revealing the history of the vehicles' motion as well as their current position. The hues used for each type of vehicle were modified so layers of dark and light would continually interact.

These various interpretations of the *MicroImage* process led me to thinking more about representation. While as an artist I am principally interested in the construction of the process, they must be made palpable to be experienced. I had made some assumptions in the initial software, print, and animated interpretations that I now began to reconsider. I had chosen to work only with the minimal representation of the line to hopefully expose the process without imposing extraneous

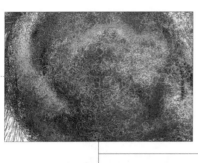

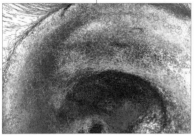

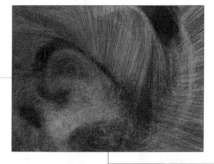

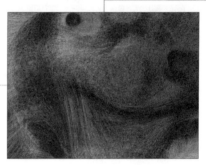

MicroImage animation on DVD, 2003

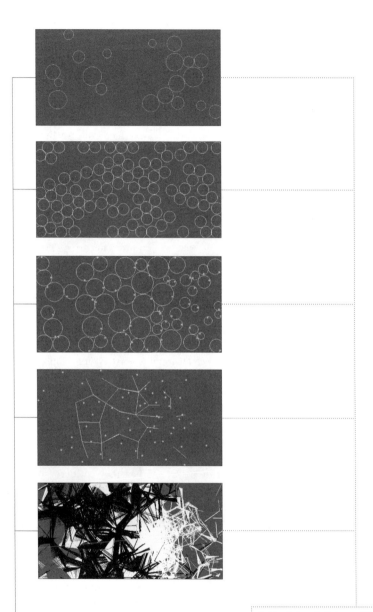

Articulate sketches, 2004. Software
explorations working toward the
Articulate software

visual adornment, but there are many different and valid ways to represent these processes, such as text representation of the algorithms (computer code written in C++) or data that is produced as the program executes. In addition, there are many ways of displaying the vehicles. It is possible, for example, to make their sensors and bodies more explicit.

Evolving a Process

....

While many people have a basic understanding of the steps involved in creating a painting or novel, very few have any idea what is involved in creating a work within the software medium. Using another of my works, *Process 4*, as an example, I follow the evolution of one process from initial conception through many stages of development. Rather than focusing on the different ways of interpreting a process, I reveal the modifications and changes within the period of refinement.

Since 2001, I have collaborated with Ben Fry in developing a software application called Processing, a programming language and environment for artists and designers.[3] On one level, Processing is a software sketchbook, a tool for getting ideas for software out of your head and into code as quickly as possible. The application environment is minimal, containing only a text editor and toolbar to enable the code to be run, stopped, saved, or exported. We developed Processing because we thought we could develop a better tool for creating our research and could simultaneously develop a better environment for teaching concepts of software and interaction within design and art schools. I have been using it extensively for making sketches for more complex works in software.

Process 4 emerged from a simple idea—to give software elements the behavior of maintaining their own "personal" space. When they overlap with another shape, they move away so they are no longer touching. I consider this a basic pattern of living organisms and was curious to see how it translated into a simplified, dynamic simulation. I began by writing code where I could move the software elements around the screen, and when I deposited one on top of another, they both moved away; the next step was to give them constant motion, bringing the screen into perpetual motion, with no two elements overlapping because they turn away as soon as they touch one another; I was not able to properly see their behavior because the information related to their turning was not shown, so I made their direction visible as a yellow dot; I then began drawing a line between the centers of two elements as they are touching and I stopped drawing the circumference of the circles; every visual element was then removed except the lines, and the software was modified so they accumulate onto the screen. The final stage of *Process 4* within Processing used three colors to represent short, medium, and long lines and began with the elements in different configurations to encourage the pattern to develop in different directions. This was the extent to which I could explore the idea in Processing, so I moved to the C++ language to get a different view.

Articulate sketches, 2004. Refinement of
the earlier software sketches

Articulate sketch, 2004. Further
refinement of the Articulate software

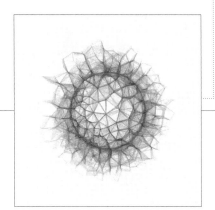

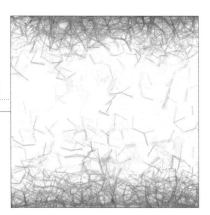

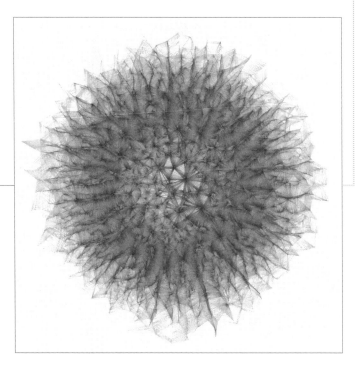

Each programming language is like a different physical material with its own properties. Processing's material properties make it quick to write programs but they display at a lower frame rate. The properties of C++ make it more complicated to write but there is potential for more resolution in time and space (the software can run faster and cover more pixels). A direct port of the *Process 4* code from Processing to C++ therefore caused it to be experienced differently, as the increased speed and resolution revealed additional properties about the system that were not visible before and opened up a new avenue of exploration. After further refinement, the software was brought to a point where it was exhibited at the [DAM] gallery in Berlin in February 2004, and then used to build the *TI installation* at the Telic Gallery in Los Angeles in spring of the same year. The piece consisted of twenty-four disks ranging in size from twelve to thirty-six inches and raised one inch above the floor, with live software visuals projected onto their surface. The audience was free to roam in and around the images, exploring a hybrid digital/physical space that evoked a tension between the organic and synthetic.

During the entire evolution of *Process 4* from its first implementation to the *TI* installation, the core algorithm remained principally the same, but the method of presenting it slowly evolved over a period of months through both technical advancements and purely aesthetic decisions. All modifications were made directly through editing the computer code. The following code was written for the display of *Process 4* in an early Processing version:

```
stroke(r, g, b);
line(x, y, others[i].x, others[i].y);
```

Compare this to an evolved method of displaying *Process 4* in C++ code:

```
glBegin(GL_LINES);
glColor4f(r/255.0, g/255.0, b/255.0, 0.0);
glVertex2f(x, y);
glColor4f(r/255.0, g/255.0, b/255.0, 0.1);
glVertex2f(others[i]->x, others[i]->y);
glEnd();
```

By looking at these code fragments, it is difficult to know precisely what the change will be. It is obvious there are differences, but exactly how they will be perceived is not possible to know until the program is run. Comparing the figures on page 173, one sees obvious differences between these two pieces of code. Each visual decision was first made intuitively and qualitatively and was then by necessity made technically and precisely in the computer code before I was able to perceive the alteration. For artists and designers used to working directly and visually with their materials, the strict constraints of programming notation can be a barrier to the flow of ideas. This barrier begins to erode with experience, but never disappears altogether.

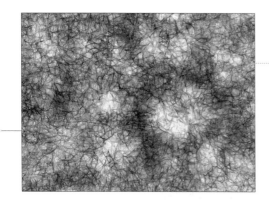

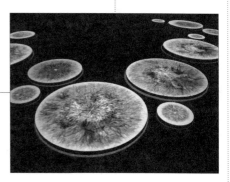

Process 4 software explorations, 2005

Articulate software, 2004. Final version exhibited at [DAM] Berlin

TI installation at the Telic Gallery, Los Angeles, 2004

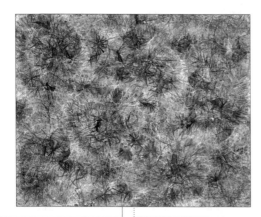

Beyond Code

The technologies I work with are continually becoming obsolete. As computers become increasingly faster and operating systems evolve, the software of the present quickly seems dated and possibly may not run directly within a few years time. I have recently been pursuing a way of working with processes and software that exists outside of the current technological framework—outside of the constraints of Java, C++, Mac OS X, or Microsoft Windows—to better focus on the concepts behind the work. This technique was inspired by the wall drawings of the artist Sol LeWitt, in which he would specify an image to be drawn on a wall through a few terse and sometimes ambiguous sentences. In LeWitt's work, the program is the English text and is executed/interpreted by a skilled draftsperson. In my previous work the program was computer code and was executed by a machine and in my new method, the program is English text, interpreted by a skilled programmer and then executed by a machine. Putting the emphasis on the text rather than the computer code creates the opportunity for multiple interpretations of the work and gives the flexibility to not feel constrained by the current state of computer technology. As an example, *Process 4* is stated as follows:

> A rectangular surface filled with varying sizes of Element 1.
> Draw a line from the centers of two Elements when they are touching.
> Set the value of the shortest line to black and the longest to white, with varying grays between.
>
> Element 1 = Form 1 + Behavior 1 + Behavior 2 + Behavior 3
> Form 1 = Circle
> Behavior 1 = Constant linear motion
> Behavior 2 = Constrain to surface
> Behavior 3 = When touching another, change direction[4]

Unique software interpretations of this text are shown in the bottom figures on page 175. I feel that the essence of the process can only be understood through comparing and contrasting these multiple interpretations and through watching the process unfold in time. Because the text is the primary representation of the process, as technology changes, the process can simply be interpreted and executed to run on the current machines, leaving the work is open for many interpretations. It is an open system from which multiple unique software objects may emerge.

Notes
....

1...Valentino Braitenberg, *Vehicles: Experiments in Synthetic Psychology* (Cambridge, MA: MIT Press, 1984).

2...Ibid., 1.

3...See http://processing.org (accessed Sept. 1, 2006).

4...In 2005 and 2006, *Process 4* was joined by *Processes 5–10*. The system of elements has slowly grown with the addition of Element 2 and Behavior 4. Each Process is a rigid starting point that fosters loose interpretations as performances, installations, prints, and projections. The code written for each Element is reusable, thus making programming similar to collage. This modular system encourages rapid experimentation and serves as a broad foundation for future work.

Climbing through Complexity Ceilings

Peter J. Bentley

Every salamander is a superhero. It is seemingly invulnerable to harm. Cutting off a leg won't stop it. It will grow a new one back, complete with bones, muscles, and blood vessels. Cutting off its tail also has no real effect. A few weeks later it will have grown a new one. Try blinding it, and it will regrow the damaged parts of its eye. No stake through the heart or silver bullet will stop our superhero salamander. Damage its heart and it'll regrow that too.

The salamander is doing more than simple healing here. It is able to regenerate parts of itself. Even when major structures have gone, it can regrow them from nothing. It is positively miraculous.

Salamanders can do these things and we can't because their cells have evolved to be a little bit different from ours. They're not the only ones. Plants are also clever in similar ways. You can amputate all of the limbs of a tree and in a couple of years it will grow a new set. Cut a leg (or "ray" as it is called) from a starfish and it will grow a new one—and the ray you've cut off will grow a new body. Snails can even regrow their entire head if they lose it.

Imagine trying to design a piece of technology that could do the same thing. A car that healed itself after a crash. A house that regrew its roof after damage from a storm. A computer that repaired itself after its circuits had been fried. Such ideas are so beyond our current abilities that they seem ludicrous. We can't design such technologies. We don't know how. Not only that, we can't even design technology that is several orders of magnitude simpler and have it work.

This article explores the idea of *complexity ceilings* and show how traditional design is failing for complex solutions. It also outlines some investigations into nature's technology: examples of computational models of biology including using computers to evolve designs, to model embryological growth and immune systems, and to mimic swarms. Nature does not perform conscious design, but her designs are better than anything a human is capable of designing. We aim to discover how this happens.

Complex Computers

Modern technology is wonderful, and most of it is driven by the computer chip. According to Moore's Law, the speed of our computer processors doubles every eighteen to twenty-four months. This extraordinary rate of progress means that our mobile phones now contain computers several hundred times more powerful than the one used to control the Lunar Lander for the Apollo missions.

We are so used to seeing faster computers every year that we take such advances for granted. But we are reaching the limits of conventional silicon chips. Within a matter of a few years we will not be able to maintain the current rate of performance increases. At this point, even by connecting our best computers together as parallel supercomputers, we will not come close to the complexity of even simple animal brains. But more importantly to our major chip manufacturers, they will have lost their ability to stay in front of the competition. Their (and our) only option for achieving improvements will be to turn to nanotechnology or quantum computers. Luckily, the news is good for nano-engineering—we are beginning to master the technology to make such molecular-sized devices. But there is still a fundamental problem: how do we *design* massively complex molecular processors?

Computer processors today are already too complex for humans to design by hand. All design is performed on the computer, and much of the design is now performed by the computer. Previously created sub-designs are placed and connected automatically by software, which makes more calculations in a second than a designer could do in their lifetime. And still the design is wasteful and inefficient. Design by computer may be fast, but it's not always good.

Molecular processors could be orders of magnitude more complex—if we were capable of designing anything so complex. In fact, there are few major innovations in processor design; most advances are made by making the devices smaller, more power efficient, and by adding more of the same: packing more memory on the chip. There are no computers with radical new architectures, no fabulous new ideas that go beyond the fifty-year-old "von Neumann Architecture" (a design that every computer in the world follows). Changing it now would be too complex.

Julian Miller is a computer scientist at the University of York who is passionate about this topic:

> I think on current trends we will find that there are not enough hardware engineers on the planet to design the kind of functionality that we will need....It is very plain to me that we cannot design any machine with as many interacting complex components as there are cells in, say, an ant. We have been fooling ourselves about this for decades. We need to create ways of evolving constructive processes that create very complex and intelligent super-systems.[1]

Complex Software

But what about software? Somehow everything seems possible in code. Problems are delicately pulled apart by master dissectors, and solutions are formed that magically instruct the computer to perform the necessary tasks. A good programmer is a virtuoso performer; his masterpieces are works of art as beautiful to comprehend as any concerto or poem.

Sadly, software is rarely written by virtuoso programmers any more. Code is now becoming "bloatware"—inefficient, slow, and containing vast quantities of old, out-of-date code (legacy code, as it is known). Software companies have opted for the stupid model for software design: add more features to the product. It's like starting with a bad car and adding more and more new things to it until it can barely be driven, despite the ultra-fast new engine under the hood. Some might argue that this sounds familiar—are our laws not created in a similar way? But this inefficient, cumulative build-up of unnecessary code is not what we see in art, or in biology. The best art is radical, new, and simple in concept. And in nature, although the genes of living creatures are written in a cumulative manner, efficiency is still paramount, so poor genes are ruthlessly pruned away. Life cannot compete if it is inefficient.

The complexity ceiling is an important reason for the downfall of code. Software is now so complex that not even a huge team of well-trained programmers can get a handle on how it all works—or indeed *if* it all works. There are so many separate elements—subroutines, modules, files, variables—all of which interact with each other in so many different ways, that it is simply beyond our abilities to cope. So, current software is not delivered as a fully working product. Rather, it's delivered and then continuously updated with "service packs" or "upgrades" to overcome the bugs in the original code. Sadly, each fix usually introduces more bugs, which also require fixing, which introduces more bugs, and so on.

Maintenance costs of software are becoming so critical that IBM have begun planning their solution: the Autonomic Computing Initiative, designed to be a "systemic view of computing inspired by self-regulating biological systems."[2] The motivation is wonderful, but sadly there are few signs that IBM has found a good design so far.

Complexity Going Wrong

It's not just computer hardware and software that is becoming over-complex; we're also reaching the complexity ceiling in other areas. For example, our wars have so many weapons and so many different armies that the job of determining friend from foe in real time is becoming very difficult, especially when your enemy will sabotage any identification measures you may try to introduce. Friendly fire is a big killer in modern warfare. We also see problems in major engineering feats: space satellites have suffered from having too many separate elements including such basic problems as a mix-up between imperial and decimal measurements. And most contemporary architecture has become sufficiently complex that there can be no guarantee that it will perform its function (like the Millennium Bridge in London—a pedestrian crossing over the River Thames which, when too many people walked in step with each other, swayed so much that it had to be reinforced).

Of course, things have always gone wrong. Wheels fell off horse-pulled carriages, unsinkable ships sank, clothes fell apart. But the difference is that today things are so much more *complicated*. From a pill to a plane, technology is now so full of complexity that there is just more to go wrong. The other difference is our reliance on technology. Technology runs the world. It creates our economies, runs our car engines, helps us design drugs, allows us to talk with anyone on the planet instantly, controls our power and our water supplies. When something goes wrong today, it has the potential to affect millions, even billions, of people.

Sadly, we're already witnessing critical failures of complex systems. On August 14, 2003, 50 million people in United States and Canada were affected by the biggest power blackout in history. A minor power surge somewhere in the Midwest caused a cascade effect as computer systems failed to cope and power station after power station overloaded. Nine nuclear reactors went offline. In Cleveland, Ohio, flights were halted, commuter trains stopped mid-route, 1.5 million people faced water shortages because the pumping stations had no power. In Cuyahoga County the Governor declared a state of emergency. In Toledo, prisons were forced to switch to emergency generators. In Lansing, Michigan, the capitol was closed and all employees sent home. In Erie, Pennsylvania, hospitals were forced to switch to emergency generators and traffic jams were caused by sporadic outages. In Newark, the Governor declared a state of emergency and mobilized seven hundred National Guard troops. A million people in New Jersey were without power. In New York City, the Governor declared a state of emergency, flights and commuter trains were halted, passengers were stranded in subway cars, some under the Hudson River. People were forced to walk home in 90 degree heat. In Springfield, Massachusetts, riders were stranded on a rollercoaster at Six Flags Amusement Park. In Toronto, the transit system was shut down, flights were halted, people were trapped in elevators, and the cell phone networks were disrupted. In Ottawa, Canada, flights were halted and serious looting was reported.

One day without electricity. Now imagine what would happen if a particularly virulent computer virus managed to wipe the data on half the world's computers. Bank accounts gone, criminal records lost, transport systems halted, exam marks erased, hospital records erased, factories shut down, food distribution to supermarkets disrupted, fuel supplies cut, television and radio off-air. It wouldn't take long for societies to break down. Our reliance on technology is alarming. The ability for complex technology to fail terminally, without warning, is also alarming.

Complexity and Design
....

So why can't we design complex systems that work? Susan Stepney, Professor of Unconventional Computing at the University of York, believes the problem is caused by the way we design:

> The current kinds of design processes for mission-critical systems are based on an incorrect assumption (that the system can be "proved correct," which means the requirements and operating environment must be completely and crisply predetermined) and produce very "fragile" systems (that are provably correct within those implausibly crisp constraints, but that shatter once they move even fractionally outside).[3]

As Stepney points out, our designs are constrained and brittle. They will function only as long as the assumptions made by the designer remain true. But in a world where all technology has become increasingly connected, our designs now form part of a larger complex system. Their environments are ever-changing: cell phones must interact with other, newer cell phones; cars must safely interact with other cars, buildings must connect and interact with other buildings; water and power networks must interact with new networks and new cities; computers must interact with each other, and the separate components of the computer (the memory, arithmetic, and logic units) must interact with each other correctly; software must interact with other software, and the separate elements in each program (variables, functions, and modules) must interact together properly. Even something as ordinary as shampoo can have over thirty different ingredients that must interact with each other and your hair in order to work properly. Design is becoming complex, and it is hard to make safe assumptions about how a complex system will work—for it is inherently unpredictable.

Humans are generally not very good at complex design—that is, design of systems with multiple components that interact in unpredictable ways. Look at the game of pool, where everything is ultra-simplified to make the movement of the balls more predictable for the players. Near-perfect spheres roll on a near-perfect flat surface, with straight boundaries around the edge. Now imagine a version of the game where all the balls have different lumps on them and the table surface is made of gravel. Imagine trying to design a trick-shot where six balls collide with each other, one by one, with the last falling into a pocket—and ensuring that the result happens every time. Now try it with a hundred balls, ten people striking balls at once, and someone jumping on the table. That's what designing a complex system is like.

When designing complex systems, we have to worry about complexity theory and chaos. A complex system has too many interacting components to be predictable using conventional mathematics. Each component affects too many others, each of which affect yet more (including themselves). The network of interactions may also be dynamic as the behavior of components changes over time, defined by other interactions. Like the "butterfly effect," if one component is poorly designed and fails, it may affect the whole system in a cascade of terminal interactions.

That's a big problem for designers.

Imagine we wished to construct a computer with the intelligence of a mouse. What's the design? No one knows. No one has the slightest clue. Not even the most intelligent, fabulously famous neurologists, cyberneticists, roboteers, engineers, brain surgeons, or rocket scientists. We know there are several billion cells called neurons involved, but we don't know how each one works and we don't know how they should be connected, or how those connections should change over time. Without the design, we can't make one, so our computers remain fast, but less intelligent than a mouse.

Let's reduce our ambitions to something more manageable. Imagine we wanted to make a spaceship. A craft that can travel to another planet, launch a probe, which would land on the surface of that planet, and send back pictures. Now, there are plenty of cyberneticists, roboteers, engineers, and rocket scientists who can and have drawn designs for such a craft. Planetary explorers have been built, launched, and some have even worked, with spectacular results. But some don't make it. Despite millions spent on their design, they burn up in the atmosphere of the planet or their circuits are fried in cosmic radiation. Or they just go wrong for an unknown reason.

Our problem is that we've hit a complexity ceiling. We don't know how to design complicated artifacts that work reliably. We can't make software that works any more. We can't design towns that don't deteriorate into areas with ghettos. We can't design drugs that don't have a myriad side effects. Yet ever more complexity is generated every day.

But there's a solution all around us. The natural world is vastly more complex than anything we could ever hope to design. Even a tiny fruit fly is a miracle of nanotechnology—a flying machine just two millimetres in size that built itself and keeps itself working by processing materials in its environment. The technology of nature has solved this problem. It knows no complexity ceiling. It also knows no designer.

Complexity and Evolution

Natural systems are a million, million times more complex than our technology. Life is designed at molecular scales. Genes and proteins are nano-robots. They instruct microbots known as cells what to do and what to be. Cells are tiny machines that make copies of themselves, transform chemicals into energy, extrude substances, and perform extraordinarily diverse functions, from neuronal computer processing to building cathedral architectures inside bones. Natural systems are also a million, million times more diverse than our technology. And yet nature has harmony and balance. Nature works. It works because there are no designers and no factories. Nature works because life designs itself, builds itself, and does everything it can to stay alive and make more copies of itself. Nature uses evolution to achieve this.

Evolution is a sculpting wind that shapes the bedrock of organisms. Its unstoppable force carves new genes into the DNA of life, sculpting organisms into new forms that have new capabilities. Evolution has no guidance; no conscious design that it follows. Evolution simply *is*.

There's no magic involved. Given any entity that self-replicates imperfectly, evolution will just happen. Those entities that are better at making more copies of themselves will become more numerous. Those that are worse will become less numerous. It's common sense. And if those evolving entities are in a complex environment, and are competing for food, then evolution will change them. They will become better able to survive. As their companions become better able to compete, they become more complex—an arms race of survival strategies. Generation after generation, the unthinking force of evolution creates ever more complexity. From atomic scales to macroscopic scales, evolution manipulates and fine-tunes, exploiting vast numbers of possible strategies for survival. Fins are invented for propulsion. Brains created to control the fins. Teeth for consuming more of the environment. Eyes to detect food better. Legs and lungs to exploit land. Wings to exploit the air. There is no plan, no direction, no mind. But that doesn't stop evolution from being the best designer and engineer in the universe.

Luckily evolution is no longer a supposition or a presumption. Evolution is part of science. We have quantified, identified, and analyzed the genes that describe many organisms, including ourselves. We can trace the same genes through many organisms and identify exactly how related life is. For fast-reproducing life such as bacteria, we can even observe evolution happening—we watch as the genes mutate and new "super bugs" evolve before our eyes.

As we learn more of genes, we discover that we can transplant genes between organisms. A gene from a squid can be inserted into the genotype of a plant, and the gene still works, producing the same compound. Genetic engineering of life is happening now. Genetically modified crops are commonplace (although not always understood). Gene therapy offers the prospect of genetic disorders being cured by the insertion of a "healthy gene."

In our computer science and engineering laboratories, we use evolution in other ways. Evolutionary computation is a field of research where solutions to problems are evolved with a computer. There is no designer—the computer simply maintains populations of solutions. Those that perform better at a predefined problem have more children. Generation by generation, the solutions evolve from randomness to near-perfection. These evolutionary programs are highly successful and are commonly used for optimization and design problems. Over the years, evolution has designed new antennas, circuits, robots, engine components, timetables, schedules, and even music and art. Today, evolution is being used to create physical forms directly. Weird electronic circuits made from liquid crystal have been evolved, that exploit the properties of the material at atomic levels—something impossible for us to achieve, for we could never know or predict what those atomic-level properties might be. Snake robots with evolved brains now slither—and recover from damage when their "smart material" muscles are injured. Evolution is a powerful process that we use every day.

Evolution behaves as a clever and imaginative designer. And like any good designer, we can learn from its designs, we can learn from how it designs, and we can directly use evolution to help us design.

This is not a recent fascination for us. Humans have always used evolution. Long before we designed and manufactured our tools, all of our technology was natural. We bred cattle that could give us better meat and regular milk. We bred crops that grew more reliably and faster. We bred flowers that smelt nicer. We bred dogs and cats, birds and fish that helped us better, comforted us, or simply looked nicer to us. At no point did we sit down and design these creatures and plants. We simply picked the ones we preferred and bred them together. All we did was choose. Evolution provided the variability, the invention. The animals and plants designed themselves and made themselves.

Complexity and Development

Humans may have unwittingly (and more recently, deliberately) used evolution, but we're still missing some important tricks from nature. Life is designed by evolution, and life is *complex*. Living organisms have extraordinary capabilities compared to our primitive "high technology." We don't know how to design technology with any of these capabilities. For example, none of our technology can maintain itself. We have nothing that can find its own food and process it into energy. We also have little that can repair itself or recover from damage. Usually if our device malfunctions, either someone repairs it or the device is trashed. We certainly do not have anything that can build itself. And the idea of our technology reproducing itself seems either ludicrous or fantastical—a television having children?

Life does all of this and more. The trick it uses to achieve these feats is known as *development*. It's the process of growing, from single fertilized egg to multicellular organism. It's the cleverest computer program ever written.

Cells develop in an organism like people develop in a society. From birth we interact with our companions. Each person experiences different things, and so they develop different interests and go on to perform different jobs in our society. Should someone leave their job, their colleagues interact differently, often resulting in the recruitment of a replacement person. Cells do much the same things—they interact with each other, and they perform different jobs depending on those interactions. But instead of brains, cells have genes to tell them what to do.

Development is controlled by genes—the genes written by evolution. All genes do is create special molecules called proteins. The proteins are used as signals. Passed between cells, they control other genes, turning them on and off at the right times. In every cell we have the same set of genes, but those genes are switching on and off differently, because each cell receives slightly different protein signals from its neighbors. Proteins also control cells more directly—they tell the cells what to do, what to become, and when to do it.

With the right genes, a single fertilized egg is told to divide many times. Each resulting cell is then told to grow, move, become a muscle cell or blood cell or neuron, divide, or die. After sufficient time, a whole organism forms, often made of billions of cells. Organisms build themselves through development.

We now have computer models that analyze genes and cells and predict how they interact and develop. We are able to manipulate development in organisms and alter their forms. We are also beginning to use development in combination with evolutionary computation. We have learned that evolution without development is as limited as our own design process. Evolution with development enables ever-increasing complexity to emerge. Evolution needs no conscious guidance to create complexity—but it does need development.

Just as we have used evolution for centuries, so we can use development. We are creating a new field of computer science, known as computational development. In it, we evolve genetic instructions that emit signals. The signals control cells, telling them to grow, divide into two, move, alter their function, or die. As they develop, the cells interact with each other, helping to push each other into the right positions or pass messages to their companions. From a single cell to a complex multicellular organism, development can build the solutions designed by evolution. When cells correspond to electronic components, this equates to circuits growing themselves. When cells correspond to software commands, it equates to software growing itself. When cells correspond to robot parts, it equates to robots growing from egg to adult form.

But this is not all that we gain from such ideas. Development is not about creating an adult solution and then ceasing. In nature, development is a never-ending process that continues from the conception to the death of the organism. Every cell has the program of development contained within it, so should the organism be damaged, it "knows" how to repair that damage by regrowing new cells. If our technology builds itself using developmental processes, then it will also be able to repair itself should it become damaged. We would have circuits that could rewire themselves or develop new components; software that detects incompatibilities or bugs and rewrites itself; or robots that could reconfigure themselves into new forms that enable them to work again (and indeed, we've already demonstrated these effects in our labs). We'd also see other benefits: just as two genetically identical plants will always develop differently as they adapt themselves to their environments, so our developing technology could adapt itself to fit its environment as it grows. Development enables self-building, self-repairing, and adaptive technology.

Examples of designs evolved by computer in the Digital Biology Group, UCL:

Evolved art. Better-looking images are given higher fitnesses by a user.

Snake robot using shape memory alloys as internal muscles and an evolved finite state machine as a brain to control the muscles

Sports car evolved by a genetic algorithm. The computer evolved forms that needed to be aerodynamic in order to be considered fit.

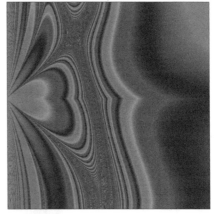

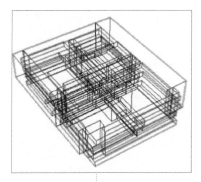

Examples of designs evolved by computer in the Digital Biology Group, UCL:

London hospital floor plan evolved by a genetic algorithm. Plans with better room layouts, which satisfy constraints and regulations, are fitter

Simulation of a Formula One car, which has had its settings optimized by a genetic algorithm to maximize its speed around the circuit

An evolved structure, constructed using rapid prototyping "3D printer" technology. This structure was evolved to withstand specific forces while being lightweight.

Research in the area is expanding rapidly. Julian Miller leads a new EPSRC research cluster known as SEEDS (Scalable, Evolvable, Emergent Developmental Systems), which he hopes will help "bring about a fundamental change in our thinking about how to design and construct complex intelligent software and hardware."[4] His own research focuses on regenerative software. His computer can evolve genetic programs that develop specific shapes, such as a French flag made from hundreds of cells. He can then damage the flag and it will regrow itself. The self-repairing ability comes free with development—Julian did not design that capability into his computer.

The computer models of development are becoming so good that developmental biologists are now taking note. And research analyzing the behavior of evolved gene regulatory networks (the patterns of gene and protein interactions) is producing some startling findings. We have now shown that evolution actually uses some of the programming tricks that we invented in our software—except that it does them better. Genes are triggered in cascades that resemble sub-routines, loops, and recursive structures. Genomes are also protected against damage—highly efficient genetic programs are built that have redundant elements in case anything is corrupted. Again, these abilities come free with evolution and development. Evolution naturally writes better code than us. Jason Lohn, head of the Evolvable Systems Group at NASA Ames, is not surprised by the benefits of computer evolution. "An important feature of these approaches," he says, "is that they produce designs that surprise and challenge humans."[5]

The combination of evolution and development is a very different form of design, which we can learn from. Evolution is not simply about function driving form. Evolution does not create forms directly—it creates developmental "building instructions" for the form. Nature's building instructions act as complex systems: networks of interactions between genes, proteins, cells, organs, and organisms produce the form of each single organism. This is how nature overcomes complexity ceilings—it makes complexity part of the solution instead of part of the problem.

Complexity and Physics

Of course it's not so easy to design using these ideas. In nature, evolution and development aren't abstract computational concepts, they are embodied, physical, chemical processes that rely on and use actual substances. DNA is a physical thing—it is a long, complicated molecule. The genes on a strand of DNA could never do a thing without the chemical interactions between cleverly designed molecules in a cell. And cells could never move, change shape, extrude substances, stick to each other, and generally collaborate to build larger morphologies if there were no laws of physics. Natural processes such as development rely on forces between cells, different levels of "stickiness," diffusion of molecules through cell walls, and a host of other very physical properties of materials to build organisms. Evolution has spent billions of years playing with these physical properties and so writes its genetic programs making assumptions that such physical properties exist. Nature doesn't just use physics, it exploits it in every possible way to ensure that organisms will be efficient.

But how do we incorporate such physics? How do we ensure our designs exploit physics as well as nature does? Can we embody evolution and development in physics? So far we know of two methods. The first is to create a computational physics within computer software and let evolutionary computation and computational development exploit it. A sufficiently complex digital universe will drive evolution and development toward useful complex solutions. One recent innovation is the use of fractals to achieve this—for fractals enable infinite levels of complexity within a computer. A fractal chemistry and fractal physics inside the computer can then be as complex as the chemistry and physics used by nature. But this will still confine evolution and development to the mind of the computer. That's fine if we are evolving software, but what if the problem is to create a physical design in the real world?

The other option is to use reconfigurable materials. We already have a special type of silicon chip known as an FPGA (field programmable gate array), which can be reconfigured to act as different physical circuits. We have evolved highly innovative circuits in these chips—circuits that exploit intrinsic molecular features in individual pieces of silicon in order to function. The next stage is underway: working with materials scientists to exploit the new collection of exotic "smart materials" that have been developed but as yet have had no application. The plan for future computer processor design is to use solid materials that can be reconfigured by development and evolution—growing processors inside them. One option might be a type of liquid crystal—it can be reconfigured to alter its optical characteristics, potentially enabling the development of optical circuits. Smart materials can also change shape: for example "shape memory alloys" can be configured to switch between different morphologies. We're already using these smart materials to make the first shape-shifting robots.

While we may confine evolution to the minds of computers some of the time to enable high-speed design, such materials will enable our evolved and grown designs to become physical, embodied objects. They will develop into physical technology that exploits the materials they are made from, just as they exploit their environment. Unlike current technology that tends to fail because the intrinsic properties of its constituent materials work against the designs, this technology could harness the intrinsic properties to help keep itself operating.

Complexity and Learning

Although natural evolution has no brain, it does learn. It tries out genetic variations, testing them in organisms, and remembers by storing what it has learned as genes on

Examples of investigations of development in the Digital Biology Group, UCL:

A developing computational embryo, with evolved genes expressing proteins that diffuse between cells, controlling the growth.

Two-dimensional reaction diffusion of two chemicals, modeled by cellular automata

Three-dimensional reaction diffusion modeled by 3D cellular automata and visualized using a ray-marching algorithm

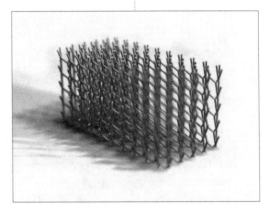

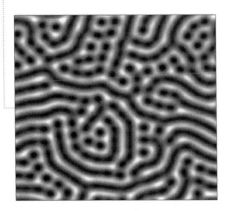

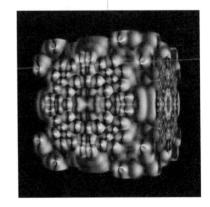

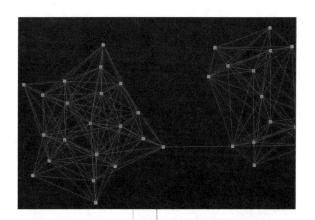

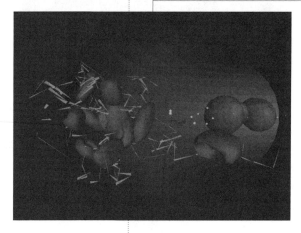

Artificial Immune System simulation by the
Digital Biology Group, UCL

Investigations of origins of hierarchical
complexity: evolved and developed
cooperating ecologies of cells linked via
spring forces

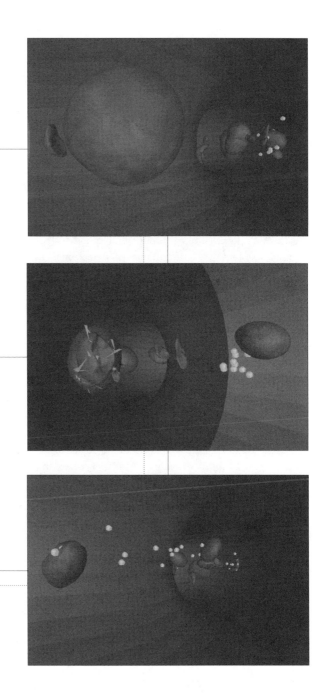

DNA molecules. Development also can be thought of as a learning process. Most living creatures are designed to react and adapt to their environments. An overworked piece of skin will thicken itself, a plant will grow different kinds of leaves where the sun is strongest, a bacterium will switch between "run" and "tumble" locomotive behaviors.

Studies of natural processes reveal many such learning systems. Our immune systems are an impressive example. Life tries to find every niche available in order to exist, and unfortunately there is plenty of space within our bodies for parasites, bacteria, fungi, and viruses to stretch their metaphorical legs. So, throughout our evolutionary history, in order to stay alive we've had to fight. Our bodies had to learn to detect and repair damage, remove invaders, and remember those invaders to make us immune next time. They had to learn to detect foreign forms of life within us that they had never experienced before, and indeed that had never existed before. And yet they must never be confused by the helpful bacteria in our guts, the food we eat, or the growing foetus within a mother's womb. Along the way, our bodies also learned how to detect malfunctions within themselves: cancerous cells proliferating wildly or immune cells attacking ourselves instead of our attackers.

To achieve these marvels, evolution created a whole collection of chemicals, organs, and cells distributed throughout our bodies. This is a wonderful example of a complex system that uses trillions of interacting elements to achieve its goal of keeping us alive. We now know enough about how this works to be very impressed by the capabilities of natural immune systems. We also know enough to create a diverse range of computer algorithms based on the workings of different aspects of our immune systems.

So computer science meets immunobiology. The result is the young but vigorous field known as Artificial Immune Systems. Inspired by the natural immune system, computer scientists now create evolving, learning, and adapting computer systems that (among many applications) can recognize patterns, detect faults, keep computer networks secure, and optimize solutions. The images show examples of an artificial immune system being developed as an immersive virtual reality work of art. Its dynamics and behaviors emerge from the interactions of its components. Although impossible to mathematically analyze or predict, its behavior can be modeled.

Learning is not just within us, it is everywhere in nature, including beneath our feet.

Complex, organized behavior is common among insects, as entomologists will tell us. Termites, ants, wasps, and bees act as coordinated units where the individual is unimportant but the whole is all-important. Just as the separate neurons in brains act together to produce thought, so the separate insects act together. Even though an ant may be as simple as a robot with seven rules to govern its entire repertoire of behavior, an ant colony is capable of behaviors as complex as any big-brained mammal. And once again, the same principles work within our computers. Using large numbers of simple programs or agents, we have shown that "swarm intelligence" can be used to perform planning and solve scheduling problems. More recently, researchers have created digital ant colonies within computers, designed to move and follow pheromone trails in the same way as the ants in our physical world. These digital ants have been used to solve "traveling salesman problems"–finding the shortest and most efficient paths between different destinations. They have also been used to optimize design problems by wandering in a digital universe where good designs correspond to places in a landscape that the ants find. Current work at the author's Digital Biology Group is investigating the use of swarms for nanotechnology: using evolution and developmental ideas to help design a learning controller which will control a swarm of nano-particles and ensure that a desirable form is built.

Conclusion

The technology of humankind has leapt forward at an extraordinary rate, particularly since the "computer revolution." But the rate of advancement cannot be maintained using conventional design techniques. Our ambitions are already beyond our capabilities. Conventional methods are causing designs to fail catastrophically every day. We need to look toward nature's methods. We need to learn how evolution designs organic forms, how development builds, maintains, and repairs those forms, and how the physical properties of the materials used in the designs is exploited, down to molecular scales. We need to learn how complex designs fail when they become caught up in undesirable complex systems. But above all, we need to understand how natural complex systems can be used to help us create our complex designs.

Bibliography

....

Philip Ball (1999) *The Self-Made Tapestry. Pattern Formation in Nature.* Oxford University Press, New York.

Jonathan Bard. (1992) *Morphogenesis. The cellular and molecular processes of developmental anatomy.* Cambridge University Press.

Peter J. Bentley (2004) Software Seeds: The Garden Where Perfect Software Grows. Feature in *New Scientist.* 6 March. Reed Business Information Ltd. (London). pp. 28–31.

Peter J. Bentley (2004) Fractal Proteins. In Genetic Programming and Evolvable Machines Journal, Kluwer Academic Publishers, London. v5, 71–101.

Peter J. Bentley (2002). *Digital Biology. How nature is transforming our technology and our lives.* Simon & Schuster (USA Hardback). ISBN: 0743204476.

Peter J. Bentley (Ed.), (1999) *Evolutionary Design by Computers.* Morgan Kauffman Pub.

Peter J. Bentley and David W. Corne (Eds.), (2001) *Creative Evolutionary Systems.* Morgan Kauffman Pub.

Behravan, R., Bentley, P. J. and Carlisle, R. (2004) Exploring Reaction-Diffusion and Pattern Formation for Conceptual Architecture. Book chapter submission for Morel, P. and Feringa, J. (Eds.) *Computational Architecture.* (DAPA, French Governmental Fund for the Art, Archilab, FKBK). 2004.

Eric Bonabeau, Marco Dorigo, Guy Theraulaz (1999) *Swarm Intelligence.* Oxford University Press Inc, USA.

Terry Bossomaier and David Green (1998) *Patterns in the Sand. Computers, Complexity and Everyday Life.* Helix Books.

George A. Cowan, David Pines and David Meltzer (Eds.) (1994) *Complexity. Metaphors, Models and Reality.* A Proceedings volume in the Santa Fe Institute Studies in the Science of Complexity, Perseus Books, Reading Massachusetts.

Charles Darwin (1859) *The Origin of Species.* Penguin Classics (1985).

Richard Dawkins (1989) *The Extended Phenotype.* Oxford University Press.

Richard Dawkins (1991) *The Blind Watchmaker.* Penguin Books.

Gary William Flake (1999) *The Computational Beauty of Nature. Computer Explorations of Fractals, Chaos, Complex Systems, and Adaptation.* A Bradford Book, MIT Press.

Murray Gell-Mann (1998) *The Quark and the Jaguar. Adventures in the Simple and the Complex.* Abacus Books, London.

Eric Goles and Servet Martinez (Eds.) (1999) *Cellular Automata and Complex Systems.* Kluwer Academic Publishers.

Tim Gordon and Peter J. Bentley (2004) Evolving Hardware. Book chapter for Zomaya, A. (Editor) Handbook of Innovative Computing. Springer-Verlag (USA). 2004.

James Haefner (1996) *Modeling Biological Systems. Principles and Applications.* Chapman and Hall, International Thompson Publishing.

Haroun Mahdavi, S. and Bentley, P. J. (2004) Innately adaptive robotics through embodied evolution. To appear in Proc. of Robosphere 2004, the 2nd Workshop on Self-Sustaining Robotic Systems, NASA Ames Research Center, Nov 9–10, 2004.

John Holland (1998). *Emergence. From Chaos to Order.* Oxford University Press.

Steve Jones (1994) *The Language of the Genes.* Flamingo.

Stuart Kauffman (1993). *The Origins of Order. Self-Organisation and Selection in Evolution.* Oxford University Press.

Kaewkamnerdpong, B. and Bentley, P. J. (2004) Perceptive Particle Swarm Optimisation. Submitted to The Seventh International Conference on Adaptive and Natural Computing Algorithms (ICCANGA 2005), 21–23 March 2005, Coimbra, Portugal.

James Kennedy, Russ Eberhart, Yuhui Shi (2000) *Swarm Intelligence.* Morgan Kaufmann Pub.

Sanjeev Kumar. and Peter J. Bentley (Eds.) (2003) *On Growth, Form and Computers.* Academic Press.

Julian F. Miller and Peter Thomson, "Beyond the Complexity Ceiling: Evolution, Emergence and Regeneration", Workshop on Regeneration and Learning in Developmental Systems, GECCO 2004.

Nicosia, G., Cutello, V., Bentley, P. J. and Timmis J. (Eds.) (2004) Artificial Immune Systems. Proceedings of the Third International Conference (ICARIS 2004). Lecture Notes in

Computer Science 3239. Springer-Verlag. ISBN 3-540-23097-1.

William E. Paul (Ed.) (1991) *Immunology: Recognition and Response*. Readings From Scientific American. W. H. Freeman and Company, New York.

J. M. Slack (1997) *From Egg to Embryo. Regional Specification in Early Development*. 2nd Edition. Cambridge University Press.

Susan Stepney. (2002) Critical Critical Systems. FASeC'02, London, December 2002. LNCS 2629. Springer, 2003.

Ian Stewart (1997) *Does God Play Dice? The New Mathematics of Chaos*. Penguin Books.

Lewis Wolpert et al. (1998). *Principles of Development*. Oxford University Press.

Krysztoff Wloch and Peter J. Bentley (2004) Optimising the Performance of a Formula One Car using a Genetic Algorithm. In Proc. of Eighth International Conference on Parallel Problem Solving From Nature Birmingham, 18–22 September 2004.

Notes

. . . .

1...Quoted in Peter Bentley, "Software Seeds," http://www.cs.ucl.ac.uk/staff/p.bentley/softwareseeds.html (accessed Aug. 10, 2006).

2...IBM Autonomic Computing, http://www.research.ibm.com/autonomic/ (accessed Sept. 14, 2006)

3...Ibid.

4...Quoted in Peter Bentley, "Software Seeds," http://www.cs.ucl.ac.uk/staff/p.bentley/softwareseeds.html (accessed Aug. 10, 2006).

5...Ibid.

Multi-National City: Inside Outsourcing

Reinhold Martin

Multi-National City (MNC) is the name we give to the city of corporate globalization. In the research from which this text is excerpted, we follow three architectural itineraries through three such cities and their histories: Silicon Valley, New York's internal suburbias, and Gurgaon, a new corporate city outside of Delhi.[1] These itineraries in turn follow the feedback loops of globalization in both space and time. Multi-National City therefore refers to each city individually, as well as to the single, pulsating "mega-city" to which they all belong. This city, made up of diffuse and constantly changing networks, comes into focus with each feedback loop only to fade into another. In that sense it offers a challenge to paradigms established by works like *Learning from Las Vegas* and *Delirious New York*, which look to single cities in order to discern possible futures for both architecture and urbanism. Understanding the MNC also requires an understanding of contemporary corporate space in general, while the conjunction of the two demands an answer to a question that is often left open by historical research: What is to be done?

We use the term "multi-national" here rather than the more current "transnational" or the more conventional "global" to emphasize the internal multiplicities to be found within what is often understood as a homogeneous monoculture that spreads through the circuitry of corporate globalization. Such multiplicities often take the form of displacements, where an apparently homogeneous "space of flows" turns out to be full of holes, gaps, and discontinuities.[2] For example, a figure that seems anachronistic or untimely in one context—as the term "multi-national corporation" might seem in the United States (with its overtones of the 1970s)—is all too timely in another. Thus in postmodern India, land of the acronym, the term "multi-national corporation" is commonly shortened to MNC, which inscribes the dreamspaces of an emergent globality materialized in shopping malls, call centers, and office buildings in cities like Gurgaon.

And so we borrow the letters MNC while insisting on their ambiguity—since the Multi-National City, with its promise of new freedoms for some, remains shadowed by the Multi-National Corporation, much like delirious, metropolitan New York was in an earlier era shadowed by big business. That is what globalization is: a simultaneous coupling and distancing in both space and time, in which, as the anthropologist

Martin/Baxi Architects, Multi-National
City

DLF City, Gurgaon

DLF City, Gurgaon. Aerial view looking
toward New Delhi

Hafeez Contractor, DLF Princeton Estates,
DLF City, Gurgaon

Arjun Appadurai once put it, "your present is their future."[3] In other words, under globalization the world is anything but "flat," and what appears homogeneous and smooth is actually heterogeneous and fractured. These fractures mark differentials of all kinds, including structural exclusions that come into focus with respect to the very real "imagined communities"—like "you" (or "us") and "them"—conjured by and in the MNC. For the MNC is also a continuous interior, a network of airports, parking garages, office lobbies, elevators, and living rooms in which, from one perspective, "you" are on the inside and "they" are on the outside, while from another, "they" are inside and "you" are outside, perhaps trying to get in. This topological ambiguity is concretized in the case of the Indian software engineer working in Gurgaon who obtains a Resident Alien visa (a green card) through her company to work for that same company in the United States, an act that reaffirms borders even as it seems to erase or overcome them.

And what about architecture here? Gurgaon is a burgeoning "cyber-city" (to use the Indian terminology again) that has sprung up over the past decade near the airport, <u>on the semi-rural outskirts of New Delhi</u>, which was itself once on the semi-rural outskirts of Delhi proper ("old" Delhi), having now been encircled by the dense sprawl of massive urbanizations. According to its developers, Gurgaon harbors the largest privately owned conurbation in Asia: a series of sprawling, irregular enclaves that together cover about 1,200 hectares (3,000 acres) and go by the name of DLF City. As a set of non-contiguous spatial units, or islands, held together by an institutional identity or brand—DLF, or Delhi Land Finance Group—DLF City is the MNC in microcosm. And like the MNC, the DLF Group is in the business of constructing both buildings and cultural imaginaries.

DLF City is a private city financed by speculative capital. In early public relations materials, its developers celebrated what they called the city's "walk to work concept: making global corporates feel at home," a concept often heard but "rarely possible in today's congested metropolis." According to the DLF Group, not only does this reduce transportation costs, it "reduces executive stress" and thus increases productivity, while on the home front "it makes for much fuller family life," since "time available with the family is a lot more than would otherwise be possible."[4] Hidden in these proclamations is a tension, in which the bonds of the traditional, extended Indian family are threatened by the demands of commuting to the new utopia of the office park, and by the multiple allegiances of corporate life. This occurs at both the level of the so-called executive (the implied patriarch), and that of the offspring, whose new job at the call center down the road may require her to work evenings. Since, in the Multi-National City, not only is your present their future, but your day is their night—the waking hours, that is, of potential credit card customers on the other side of the globe.

DLF City consists of five phased residential enclaves, a series of corporate office complexes, and a series of shopping malls. The gated enclaves go by such names as DLF Windsor Court, DLF Hamilton Court, DLF Regency Park, DLF Richmond Park,

DLF Belvedere Towers, DLF Belvedere Place, DLF Silver Oaks, DLF Wellington Estate, DLF Oakwood Estate, DLF Ridgewood Estate, DLF Beverly Park, DLF Carlton Estate, and DLF Princeton Estate. To be sure, such mass-mediated names connect these objects to other objects in places like suburban New Jersey, where new condominium developments in the greater Princeton area offer an independent, homeowning lifestyle to the expanding class of international, English-speaking technical workers trained in India's elite technological and management institutes. Both inside and outside India, such economic immigrants are part of a larger construction of the multinational imaginary called the NRI, or Non-Resident Indian. The much-vaunted "opening up" of the Indian economy during the 1990s saw tax breaks for NRI investors. And so, in addition to the upwardly mobile, new middle class who imagine themselves as "walk-to-work" executives, among the clientele for DLF City is the NRI, for whom apartment units in Princeton Estates may represent both a potential investment in a rising real estate market and a kind of displaced homecoming—a base from which to visit the family in Delhi, while still maintaining a distance.

Other such avatars in Gurgaon include the DLF Square Tower, the DLF Gateway Tower, and the DLF Plaza Tower. These are surrounded by assorted shopping malls and are in close proximity to that all-important lifestyle amenity for walk-to-work executives unable to tolerate their family for very long: a golf course. Adjacent to DLF City Phase V, the DLF Golf and Country Club come complete with five lakes, "greens that play true," and a downloadable application form that helps construct the very golfers it serves by offering varying rates to "overseas corporate members," NRIs, individual residents, individual expatriates, and corporations, though it is unclear whether these categories are in fact mutually exclusive.[5]

Also adjacent to DLF City Phase V on Vishwakarma Road, though not technically part of DLF City proper, is the General Electric call center. Dedicated mainly to the back-office marketing and service operations of GE Capital, the call center is representative of the strange topologies of outsourcing. Today's anguished debates about sending so-called American jobs overseas miss the point, since a key job description for many call center operators is the ability to produce a simulacrum of the "American," overseas. Consider the following account from the weekly India Today. Meghna is a twenty-three-year-old call-center operator somewhere in Gurgaon. When her phone rings, she becomes "Michelle." The caller is in Philadelphia, asking for a credit extension:

> Meghna is unruffled. Months of training, which included watching Hollywood blockbusters to pick up a wide variety of American accents and reading John Grisham thrillers to clear any linguistic obstacles, have paid off. Her computer screen even flashes the weather at Philadelphia as she tells a caller what a perfect day it is. Meghna signs off saying, "Have a good day." Outside her window it is pitch dark.[6]

This is the true meaning of outsourcing at the global scale: the production and reproduction of national and cultural identity on the *inside* of an *exterior* space—inside the call center, out there in Gurgaon, at night. In that sense, the call center operator is the prototypical subject of the Multi-National City, a cyborg who switches identities by plugging into technological networks that scramble time and space into a topological knot.

In the American imagination as well as on the ground, cities like Bangalore in southern India, with its International Tech Park Ltd., or ITPL, materialize the specter of outsourcing. But whether in Bangalore or Gurgaon, outsourcing's strange topologies would not be possible without the technical infrastructure that provides the uplink—in the case of Bangalore's ITPL, the prominently placed satellite dish that, like the building's stone and glass curtain walls, fulfills both a functional and symbolic role simultaneously. This role is prefigured, perhaps, by the cryptic symbolism of Le Corbusier's sculptural dome atop the Assembly building at Chandigarh, city of Nehru's technological dreams—the same nation-building dreams that produced the reality of India's Institutes of Technology (founded in the 1950s), from which the new technological class has largely emerged. There is also a large satellite dish poised prominently atop the GE Capital call center in Gurgaon, signaling the building's status as a machine for producing multi-nationals of all kinds. On the inside, the cubicle space is divided into territories corresponding to regions serviced: North America, Europe, Africa, and so on. The globe, internalized.

The interiors of GE Capital were designed by the Delhi-based firm of Framework Interiors, whose production was singled out in 2002 by the periodical *Architecture + Design* as exemplifying "Multinational Design for the Multinational Mind."[7] And indeed, the mindset of Framework Interiors is no different from that of their American counterparts: applying Silicon Valley–style office planning methods such as the relaxed, "open" office with designated social areas; or "hotelling," in which workers "plug and play" into different workstations on a daily basis, as well as "internal branding," a packaging of the corporation from the inside-out designed to induce brand-loyalty in the employees rather than the customers.

The architect of the GE Capital call center in which Framework Interiors exercised their craft was India's most prolific—and arguably most famous—practitioner: the inimitable Hafeez Contractor. By mid-2004, Hafeez (as he is generally called) had designed 4 million square feet of residential space, 2.5 million square feet of commercial space, and half a million square feet of shopping for the DLF Group. In more ways than one, Hafeez is a multi-national architect; his firm's PR materials identify him as holding a Master of Science in Architecture and Urban Design from the United States—in fact the degree is from Columbia University, which probably makes Hafeez that university's most prolific architectural alumnus. But in terms of the cultural capital out of which the Multi-National City is built, it remains more important in the Indian context to identify oneself as having studied "abroad" than to name the specific institution. And like many of the founders of India's burgeoning information technology (IT) industry to which DLF City caters, Hafeez returned to India after his studies, foregoing the temptations (or hardships) of life as an NRI in New York and founding his own practice in Mumbai (then still officially called Bombay) in 1982.

Hafeez Contractor, GE Capital call center, with DLF Princeton Estates in the background

Hafeez Contractor, DLF Square Tower

Hafeez Contractor, DLF Gateway Tower (left) and Ericsson headquarters (right)

So despite the inclination of Western architects to regard such Eastern developments as Gurgaon as emerging spontaneously out of the exotic, ahistorical jungles of globalization—Shanghai as "primitive hut," to name another—these cities are nothing if not historical. Hafeez's unapologetic postmodernism is in many ways a remixed echo of earlier postmodernisms that Eurocentric architects used to call historicist. Looming large over private, postmodern cities such as Gurgaon is also the still-present ghost of Le Corbusier and the hulking mass of Chandigarh—the modernist promise of a new future emanating from the recently decolonized public sector. In that sense, Hafeez materializes a kind of Corbusian alter ego who will build in any style whatever, thereby refusing the reactions to international modernism that advocate a more "authentically" Indian architecture. As a result, Hafeez's postmodernism and the televisual image of the West that it projects (a kind of architectural equivalent to pan-Asian Star TV) are surely agents of endocolonization, or colonization from the inside. But they also deflect the jargon of authenticity associated with another postmodernism, that of national identity, in a betrayal of the "Indianness" advocated by the far right. While in actuality, in Gurgaon and beyond, these two essentialisms—that of a national style and that of a global one—are two sides of the same coin.

In addition to the GE Capital call center, among Hafeez's output in DLF City proper is the DLF Square Tower, with an upside-down pyramid (the DLF logo) at its base—the figurative skyscraper top that once marked the skyline of "delirious New York," now inverted to become the ubiquitous emblem of the new, Multi-National City: a glass atrium. The atrium features prominently in other Hafeez buildings in Gurgaon, such as the Ericsson headquarters. These atriums are monuments to the MNC's relentlessly empty interiority. But DLF City is not without a skyline. Not only does the bulk of the DLF Square Tower hover over the still-vast fields formerly tended by villagers now rendered nearly invisible by its looming postmodernity; the entrance to DLF City, and to the new districts of Gurgaon into which it is embedded, is marked by Hafeez's DLF Gateway Tower, completed in 1999. When it opened, the DLF Group duly proclaimed this building's state-of-the-art technology, including "The 100% power back-up facility [that] makes sure that office efficiency is maximised at all times,"[8] a claim that reminds us that the politics of the MNC is often a politics of infrastructure.

Many Indian cities, and especially Delhi, are plagued by vast, sometimes daily power outages, due to a power generation and distribution infrastructure stretched well beyond its capacities by massive urbanization and both authorized and unauthorized (or pirated) loads. In residential neighborhoods, the use of individual backup generators in the event of a power outage is widespread, to the degree that the economic makeup of a given neighborhood is starkly visible during a blackout by virtue of whose lights are on and whose are off. Industry has followed suit, offering not only backup generators in structures like the DLF Gateway Tower but also the class prestige that goes along with them, analogous to the westernized names of the DLF housing estates—or housing "colonies," as they used to be called with uncanny precision.

Another architectural status symbol is the mirrored glass curtain wall that covers half of what the DLF Group calls Gateway Tower's "futuristic exterior." Again: your past is their future—or perhaps it's the other way around. One commentator writing in India's *Architecture + Design* describes (with tongue in cheek) a mirrored glass, spherical office building in Bangalore as "a globe building for a 'global' corporation," and therefore a Venturian "duck," albeit absent the usual irony.[9] Gurgaon has its own version, minus the spherical form: the Global Business Park, designed by Sikka Associates and completed in 2002. But does that mean that this and other such buildings are decorated sheds—where the equation "glass = global" is applied as mere billboard to the otherwise unremarkable shell of the otherwise unremarkable office building?

Clients in India's IT parks have been known to request a specific percentage of curtain wall for their buildings. But that does not necessarily qualify these buildings as decorated sheds, since the curtain wall is more than merely a sign with structure behind; it is a surface with specific topological properties—a two-sided sign. These enigmatic mirrors both reflect and fold the Multi-National City back onto itself, thus doubling up both its strange exteriority and its strange intimacy. In effect, they defeat the logic of inside and outside, us and them, even as they reproduce it. This is not merely a matter of a false transparency, a false universality at once offered and refused, where you can see out but you can't see in, or vice versa. Nor is it a matter of glass architecture as "global" architecture. It is a matter of that mathematical property familiar to all digital architects known as the "normal." Normal to one side of the mirror is its reflective opacity; normal to the other, its transparency. This double valence is doubled many times over throughout the MNC, and so it may not be entirely inappropriate that another acronym, MBA, or Martin/Baxi Architects, has since proposed to double up DLF City on the inside, and thus to turn this city of upside-down towers inside-out.[10]

At the southern extremity of Gurgaon sits DLF City Phase V, the site of Carleton Estates and Princeton Estates, with the GE Capital call center adjacent and, as of early 2004, yet another new shopping mall on the horizon. Across the road there is the golf course: the dreams of corporate golf surrounded by the dubious promise of a fully incorporated life, where going global really means looking in the mirror and seeing yourself inside-out, upside-down—as Meghna in the call center becomes "Michelle." But in 2004 DLF Phase V remained incomplete, so MBA decided to remedy that, stepping in before Hafeez Contractor and others had a chance to seal the deal on the future of the MNC. To complete DLF Phase V, the first thing MBA proposed was to reduce the density—a counterintuitive move, perhaps, for architects committed to urbanity. But where the floor area ratio (FAR) of the existing portion of Phase V is 2.3, MBA proposed a reduction to 1.0, in recognition of the imperatives hiding behind DLF's marketing fantasy of the "walk-to-work" lifestyle and the backup generator:

Martin/Baxi Architects, Feedback: DLF (DLF City Phase V), Gurgaon. Site plan

Feedback: DLF (DLF City Phase V). Typical building, with solar array/parking lot

Feedback: DLF (DLF City Phase V). Atrium

Feedback: DLF (DLF City Phase V). Typical building, layers

Le Corbusier, Le Modulor (left); Le Corbusier, Le Modulor, mathematical/ geometrical "error" (center); Martin/Baxi Architects, Le Modulor, revised (right). Drawing by Urtzi Grau

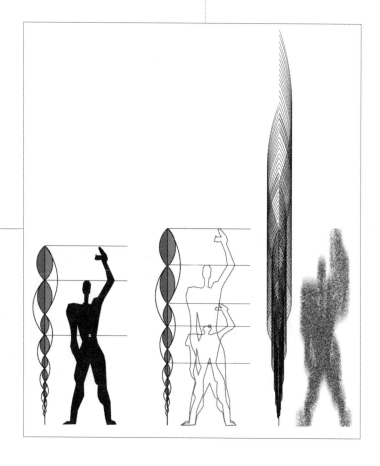

the politics of energy and infrastructure that lie behind all so-called modernization. Since if there is anything that distinguishes Gurgaon's urbanity from, say, that of Silicon Valley (with its FARs of .5 and below), it is this formula, which ultimately comes down to parking.

In MBA's proposal ("Feedback: DLF"), the irregular property outline of DLF Phase V is subdivided into thirty circular, secondary sectors, each its own closed world. Each of the circles is paved, while the interstitial landscape between them is left in its original state—inevitably to be filled in with the huts and squalor reserved for those condemned to service India's service economy. At the center of each is a depression, which serves as a sunken entry plaza to the building placed there. The remainder of the paved surface area is reserved for a zero-sum game of ecology and economy: a fixed amount of area which the occupants of each circle can use in one of two ways—as parking or as solar energy source for backup power—but not both. Thus in each, a different pattern of solar panels and parking spaces develops, reflecting the differing priorities and politics of each circle, with densities also varying from circle to circle.

The size of each building varies proportionately with that of its circle. Each is a cube, with a cubic, voided atrium at its center. Each cube is punctured on each of its six sides with a mirrored vortex: the "global," glass curtain wall turned inside-out and sucked into the deepest interior of each object. This internalized atrium is wrapped in one-way mirrored glass with its normals reversed. In the city of mirrored globes, you can look out but you can't look in; here you can look in (to the atrium) from each unit, but you can't look out.

Each building is composed of three layers, articulated at three different scales. On the outside, a high-resolution screen wall of multicolored pixels; in from that, a medium-resolution screen in another array that separates the units from the external circulation; and inside of that, a low-resolution array of volumes that serve as both service cores and structure, subdividing each floor into different-sized units. Together these screens recall both Le Corbusier's standardized brises-soleil at Chandigarh and the clichéd, Orientalized screens famously applied over a glass box by Edward Durell Stone at the U.S. Embassy in New Delhi to signify "context." At Chandigarh, the screens and other elements of the capitol complex used a revised version of Le Corbusier's Modulor proportioning system, which "corrected" the system's original 1/6,000 discrepancy between mathematics and idealized geometry. In contrast, at DLF City Phase V, the distribution of pixel-units in each screen is programmed and generated digitally to amplify—rather than to mask—Le Corbusier's original error.

The result is an array of multicolored cubes, each a different size, each with a different pixilated facade of multicolored noise, and a different distribution of volumes on its interior. Each cube in each circle thus contains both a neutralization and a surplus of identity: each has a different location, different size, different solar pattern, and different facade pattern, inside and out. Same difference. Circulation through the complex occurs in circles. At each overlap there is a spherical, digital

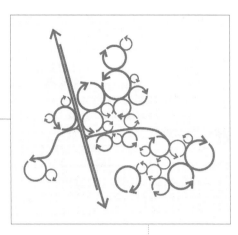

Feedback: DLF (DLF City Phase V). Site
circulation

Feedback: DLF (DLF City Phase V)

sign displaying a color-coded gradient, indicating which sector you are about to leave and which you are about to enter. In place of neocolonial nomenclature like Beverly Park or Princeton Estates, there is only color, digitally generated from the numerical average of all those other colors distributed on the respective building's facade.

This brings me to a brief word about "distributed form" and digital "network practices," specifically with respect to their potential impact on professional practice. Here, architects and urbanists must raise the stakes. They must stop worrying about how to become better entrepreneurs in the global marketplace and take responsibility once again for their share in imagining other, collective futures, even—or especially—if that means acknowledging all the ambiguities inherent therein. This responsibility is the very definition of professional practice, "networked" or otherwise. "Architecture or Revolution," someone once said. With respect to the MNC, we have chosen not to choose. Instead, we reorganize reality into new feedback loops that may or may not provide a way out. There are no guarantees. Utopian realism, you might call it.

At first glance there might seem to be little that is "real" about MBA's proposal for DLF City Phase V. Nor might there be anything evidently "utopian" about it. It might even seem dystopian, or rhetorically ironic. But this would overlook an elementary fact that is built into the concrete, stone, and glass of DLF City: what we can imagine is real. That is, the status quo is partly defined by a capacity (or lack thereof) to imagine alternatives to it. In that sense, the most terrifyingly real aspect of the MNC is its imagined—indeed, its projected—sense of inevitability. The MNC *as it already exists* is a *project*. And MBA's DLF City Phase V is a counter-project, a contribution to the cultural imaginary whose realism takes the form of an enigma: If this is a possible future extrapolated from an actually existing city, where are we going? But it is also utopian in that it attempts, via a range of topological reversals made available by the MNC itself, to turn this very question back on itself and ask: Who, in the end, is this "we," this subject of history that haunts the continuous interiors—the *networks*, that is—that makes up the Multi-National City? To the extent that this second question remains open, the MNC's networks are not (yet) completely enclosed. And the task of architecture and urbanism remains to seek out their holes, their discrepancies, and their displacements: windows onto other worlds.

Notes

....

1...This essay is based on research done in collaboration with Kadambari Baxi that is forthcoming in Reinhold Martin and Kadambari Baxi, *Multi-National City: Architectural Itineraries* (Barcelona: Actar, 2007).

2...The expression "space of flows" refers to the work of Manuel Castells. See in particular Castells, *The Rise of the Networked Society* (Cambridge: Blackwell, 1996), 326–428. The MNC also differs conceptually from the "global city" as elaborated by Saskia Sassen in *The Global City: New York, London, Tokyo* (Princeton: Princeton University Press, 1991), in that the power differentials driving its circuitry draw on the discontinuities and displacements inherent in networks of all sorts, rather than simply manage them through mechanisms of command and control.

3...Arjun Appadurai, *Modernity at Large: Cultural Dimensions of Globalization* (Minneapolis: University of Minnesota Press, 1996), 31.

4...http://www.dlf-group.com, 2002. The company's website has since been modified.

5...Originally on http://www.dlf-group.com, the DLF Golf and Country Club membership policy was later moved to the Club's own website, http://www.dlfclub.com, with similar membership categories: DLF City Property Holder, DLF City Property Holder-NRI, Lessee-Resident, and Corporate Sponsored.

6...Raj Chengappa and Malini Goyal, "Housekeepers to the World," *India Today* 1, no. 46 (Nov. 18, 2002): 10.

7...Priyanka Chauhan, "Multinational Design for the Multinational Mind," *Architecture + Design* 19, no. 6 (Nov.–Dec. 2002): 148–51.

8...Originally on http://www.dlf-group.com, 2002.

9...Vijay Narnapatti, "Glass Box Slick: Dressing Up to the Corporate Image, Bangalore Context," *Architecture + Design* 19, no. 6 (Nov.–Dec. 2002): 94.

10...The Martin/Baxi Architects team for DLF City Phase V included Kadambari Baxi, Reinhold Martin, and Urtzi Grau.

Intelligence After Theory

Michael Speaks

If one were to write a history of architecture since May 1968, noting in particular the role the events that summer played in shaping contemporary practice, it would begin by recounting the passing of philosophy and the rise of "theory"—that set of mostly French, German, and Italian philosophical tracts that arrived in the United States in the late 1970s through departments of comparative literature and were disseminated to the American university system as a wonderful new mode of contemporary thought. Theory was detached from its continental origins and replanted in the U.S., where it took on a lighter, more occasional existence. Theory was portable; it could be attached to almost any field of study—film, literature, anthropology, even architecture. It carried all the punch of philosophy without the windy German preambles and recondite French qualifications—without, that is, years of study, political affiliation, or deep knowledge. Theory was a weapon of the young, the post-'68 generation, wearied by the morality and slowness of their elders who seemed so untheoretical whether they embraced or rejected theory. Theory was fast philosophy and it made its way through various sectors of the U.S. academy in the 1970s and '80s, arriving to architecture late, as Mark Wigley has so famously and so frequently pointed out.

The shift from philosophy to theory was especially important for the vanguard architects whose work and writing came to dominate scholarly journals, school curricula, and indeed much of what passed for intellectual discourse and debate in architecture from the 1970s until the late 1990s. Whether articulated in the form of Tafurian or Frankfurt school analysis or Derridean deconstruction, these theory-inspired vanguards asserted the impossibility of affirmatively intervening in a world dominated by capitalistic and/or metaphysical oppressors. Continuous critique and resistance instead guided their resolutely negative practices. But as the 1990s drew to a close, theory-vanguardism began to wither as new architecture practices better suited to meet the challenges issued by globalization arose to claim the mantle of experimentation that the vanguard, whether in philosophical or theoretical guise, had so long held. Identified as post-critical, fresh, and ideologically smooth, these practices embraced much of the market-driven world their theory-hamstrung predecessors held in contempt.

Two features in particular distinguish these new practices. The first is their pursuit of innovation. Management thinker Peter Drucker has drawn an important distinction between problem-solving and innovation that many of these post-vanguard practices have taken to heart and that architects in general would do well to better understand. Problem-solving, Drucker argues, simply accepts the parameters of a problem given, in the case of architecture, by the client. The designer is then to work within those parameters until a solution to the problem is reached—a final design. Innovation, Drucker tells us, works by a different, more entrepreneurial logic where, by rigorous analysis, opportunities are discovered that can be exploited and transformed into innovations. While problem-solving works within a given paradigm to create new solutions to known problems, innovation risks working with the existent but unknown in order to discover opportunities for design solutions that could not have been predicted in advance.[1]

Related to this, post-vanguard practices evaluate knowledge based on its usefulness for getting things done rather than on truth content as did their vanguard predecessors. Drucker argues that the accession of modern capitalism to world system status was enabled by a fundamental change whereby knowledge was no longer concerned with philosophical or religious truth but with doing, with action.[2] After World War II this transformation ushered in the management revolution and signaled the emergence of what Drucker calls "the knowledge society," a post-capitalist paradigm enabled by globalization.[3] Taking a more pessimistic view of what they prefer to call the "society of control," Michael Hardt and Antonio Negri, authors of *Empire*, the highly acclaimed neo-Marxist study of globalization and politics, nonetheless agree with Drucker's assertion that the new economic order ushered in by globalization is knowledge-based. Though states still exist as filters of power and control, Hardt and Negri argue that real command and control is now in the hands of mobile and constantly evolving global organizations free from national obligation to roam the planet in search of affiliations that provide competitive advantage.[4] No longer stored in banks of metaphysical truths, today knowledge is manifest as intelligence used to manage these organizations in a world where remaining competitive is often a matter of life and death. As Hardt, Negri, and Drucker suggest, the great ideas of philosophy and theory have given way to the "chatter" of intelligence. Philosophical, political, and scientific truth have fragmented into proliferating swarms of "little" truths appearing and disappearing so fast that ascertaining whether they are really true is impractical if not altogether impossible. No longer dictated by ideas or ideologies, nor dependent on whether something is really true, everything now depends on credible intelligence, on whether something might be true.

If philosophy was the intellectual dominant of early-twentieth-century vanguards and theory the intellectual dominant of late-twentieth-century vanguards, then intelligence has become the intellectual dominant of early-twenty-first-century post-vanguards. While vanguard practices are reliant on ideas, theories, and concepts given in advance, intelligence-based practices are more entrepreneurial in seeking opportunities for innovation that cannot be predicted. Indeed, it is their unique, produced *design intelligence* that enables them to innovate by learning from and adapting to instability. The most innovative of these new practices are thus more concerned with the "plausible truths" generated through prototyping than with the received "truths" of theory or philosophy. Plausible truths offer a way to quickly test thinking or ideas by doing, by making them, and are thus the engines for innovation rather than its final product.

The Los Angeles–based architect George Yu put it this way in response to a question about how his office conducts research:

> The traditional distinction between research and doing or making is something that's becoming blurred for us. Doing has become research and research has become doing at this point. For us, research is not something that comes before doing—it's maybe even the other way around. Doing is in fact a kind of research. But the bigger question is: Why do research in the first place? I think that the starting point for all our projects is shaped by an attempt to understand and accept the givens of the project in a really optimistic way. To understand the real parameters of the problem at hand and add something unexpected, something that the client may not have been expecting. This kind of research is an absolute necessity given that many of our recent clients were looking for someone to help them develop an organizational vision for the company.[5]

Other forms of interactive prototyping, especially those associated with 3D modeling, have transformed the way buildings are designed and built. Commenting on the use of such modeling in the design and fabrication of the Greenwich Street Project in Lower Manhattan, completed this year, Winka Dubbeldam, principal of Archi-Tectonics in New York, noted the following about the building's folded facade:

> The folds in the facade are diagonal which means the whole space folds inside out and is pulled unlike if it were a simple fold. But this can only be controlled with the kind of precision 3D computer modeling makes possible. During the design phase the slightest change in the fold—whether for code or aesthetic reasons—affected the entire building because it was all one performative system. This also meant that with fabrication everything was controlled by mathematics, by an abstract system rather than by traditional site measurements. This leads to a completely different way of building. When the pieces arrived, they all fit together like a glove. When you see this you realize there is something very beautiful about working from abstract rules. If everyone works by them, and if all the material tolerances are observed, then making the building is all about agreements, codes, notations, not about construction in the conventional sense.[6]

Prototypes create "design intelligence" by generating plausible solutions that become part of an office's overall design intelligence. Rapid prototyping and the use of scenarios, for example, enables mass production of uniqueness in which the "final" product is both the design and the array of specialized techniques invented and deployed. Commenting on the kind of design intelligence generated through the use of scenarios and rapid prototyping, Oliver Lang, of LWPAC in Vancouver, observed the following about an extremely fast-paced project then underway in China:

> The scenario exercises utilized in earlier projects have become extremely important in helping us test the building and its ability to adapt. We got the job, in fact, because of our approach to phasing and time based design with scenarios....Platform design and rapid prototyping have been invaluable in developing this aspect of the project. All the research and intelligence generation that we have been developing over the last several years is now paying off and indeed has made it possible for a small, Vancouver-based office like ours to take on such immense and complex projects as these in China.[7]

Similarly, offices like Rotterdam-based Max.1 and Crimson focus on the development of what they call "orgware," the organizational design intelligence that negotiates between the software of policy directives, zoning and legal codes, and building or infrastructural hardware. In the mid-1990s Max.1 was offered a commission to develop a master plan for Leidsche Rijn, a new town extension for the city of Utrecht. One of the first large-scale urban planning projects in the Netherlands that reflected a turn away from subsidized to market-rate housing, Leidsche Rijn required an innovative urban planning approach flexible enough to accommodate the dramatic social and economic changes then occurring in the Netherlands, but strong enough to create a new town with its own unique urban character. Working with Crimson, a research and planning office also from Rotterdam, Max.1 developed a master plan guided by what Crimson called "orgware," the organizational intelligence used to transform the "software" of public and private policy directives into the "hardware" of buildings and infrastructure. Rather than focusing their efforts on an over-designed, inflexible master plan, Max.1 instead designed a plan of negotiation that required certain things to be built while allowing, through built-in redundancies, for other elements in the plan to be sacrificed. This same approach of engendering flexibility through enforced inflexibility guided Max.1's innovative Logica plan for Hoogvliet, a suburb or Rotterdam, also developed in conjunction with Crimson. Logica, an exemplary form of design intelligence, requires stakeholders to make definitive choices about how the city will develop. The choices were designed by Max.1 after a period of rigorous analysis and were issued as a challenge to politicians and stakeholders to take immediate action. Once made, these choices become the planning infrastructure that allows other, more flexible choices at different scales to be made over time as the city is rebuilt. As Rients Dijkstra, principal of Max.1, remarked at the conclusion of the process:

> Logica has now been accepted by the city as the official planning document. All of the choices were made by the council and now cannot be changed. They are the equivalent to the large-scale projects at Leidsche Rijn. That is, they are inflexible, not negotiable. The negotiable part comes in how the choices are implemented by the city of Hoogvliet. The choices are yes-no, and once made, they are inflexible. They are

what allow things to actually get done. They are the first, necessary step that must be taken. Now the work of filling in those choices begins.[8]

Part of a one-year "design intelligence" interview series I published in *a+u* in 2003, these four examples of intelligence-based practices cannot be categorized under any existing classification system. Some design boxes, some blobs, while others script complex ballets of urban movement. Holding to no philosophical or professional truth, making use of no specialized theory, these practices are open to the influence of "chatter" and are by disposition willing to learn. Accustomed in ways that their vanguard predecessors can never be to open-source intelligence gathered from the little truths published on the web, found in popular culture, and gleaned from other professions and design disciplines, these practices are adaptable to almost any circumstance almost anywhere.

Though we live in uncertain times, one thing is certain: experimental architecture practices are no longer driven by grand ideas or theories realized in visionary form. Instead, the most influential architecture practices are today compelled by the need to innovate, to create solutions to problems the larger implications of which have not yet been formulated. This, I argue, can only be accomplished with intelligence. Otherwise design is simply a matter of completing a problem given without adding anything new. Architecture should be more ambitious than to settle for that. Each of the offices mentioned above (and there are many more) have not settled on practices focused on what Drucker calls problem-solving; they have instead developed unique design intelligences that enable them to innovate by adding something not given in the formulation of whatever problem they have been asked to solve. They are but the first wave of a remarkable change in architecture practice.

Notes
....

1...Peter Drucker, *Innovation and Entrepreneurship* (New York: Harper Business, 1985).

2...Peter Drucker, *Post-Capitalist Society* (New York: Harper Business, 1993).

3...Ibid.

4...Michael Hardt and Antonio Negri, *Empire* (Cambridge, MA: Harvard University Press, 2000).

5...Michael Speaks, "Design Intelligence: Part 2: George Yu Architects," *a+u* 388 (Jan. 2003): 150–56.

6...Michael Speaks, "Design Intelligence: Part 11: Archi-Tectonics/Winka Dubbeldam," *a+u* 398 (Nov. 2003): 190–97.

7...Michael Speaks, "Design Intelligence: Part 6: LWPAC," *a+u* 392 (May 2003): 126–32.

8...Michael Speaks, "Design Intelligence: Part 7: Max.1," *a+u* 393 (June 2003): 140–46.

Acknowledgments

Many hands went into making both the symposium and this publication possible. From sponsors to helpers, we'd like to sincerely thank all who contributed.
Special thanks to the Graham Foundation for the Advanced Studies in the Fine Arts.

Major Sponsors

College of Environmental Design, UCB Harrison Fraker
Department of Architecture, CED, UCB Mike Martin
Center for Environmental Design Research, Ed Arens
Center for Design Visualization, UCB

Sponsors

Townsend Center for the Humanities, UCB Christina Gillis
Art and Technology Colloquium, Ken Goldberg
Intel
Architecture lecture series, Roddy Creedon

CEDR

Barbara Hadenfeldt
Jonas Jarut
Kathy Kuhlman

In the CED office, PR

Nicole Avril
Sheila Dickie

Faculty

Ray Lifchez

Assistants

Laura Boutelle_ Organization and managment
Alexis Burck_ Assistant

Beau Trincia_ Assistant and exhibition coordinator
Josh Zabel_ Graphic and web design

AV
....

Joe Gouig
Carol Lai
Heidi Plais
Yen Tram
Richie Wu

Photography
....

Amy Van Nostrand

Tech Support and Webcast
....

Steve Murray
Guy Vinson
David Virgo

UC Berkeley Chapter of AIAS
....

Reza Aghababa
Dalen Gilbretch
Matt Guerena
Lourdes Juarez
Tiffany Kirk
Audrey Moon

Publication
....

Megan Carey
Clare Jacobson_ Princeton Architectural Press
Ron Nyren_ Content editor
Scott Tennant_ Princeton Architectural Press
Beau Trincia_ Assistant

Image Credits

The Architectural Brain

33tl Roneo File Cabinet, illustration from Le Corbusier, *L'Art décoratif d'aujourd'hui*, 1925. Originally in *L'Esprit Nouveau* no. 23 (1924); 33tr Courtesy Fondation Le Corbusier, Paris; 33c "Regrouping around cooperative centers," illustration from Le Corbusier, *Les trois etablissements humains*, 1945. Image from English edition, Punjab Govt., Dept. of Town & Country Planning, Chandigarh, 1979; 33b Le Corbusier Venice Hospital Project, 1964. From *Ouevre Complete*, vol. 7, 1965, 150; 35t Louis Kahn, Philadelphia Traffic Study, 1953. *Perspecta* 2 (1953); 35b Konrad Wachsmann, Airline Hangar Project, 1953, *Architecture d'aujourd'hui*, July–August 1954; 37tl Buckminster Fuller in his 1958 MoMA space frame, trade card issued by Time Life, 1985; 37b Dennis Crompton, Computer City Project, 1964. *Archigram* no. 5 (1964); 37t Courtesy of Dennis Crompton, Archigram Archives; 39t Illustration from Chermayeff and Alexander, *Community and Privacy*, 1963; 39c Archizoom, No-Stop City project, 1970. *Domus* 496 (March 1971); 39b Superstudio, Supersurface project, 1972. *Casabella* 367 (1972); 41t Digital Image © The Museum of Modern Art/Licensed by SCALA / Art Resource, NY; 41c Cedric Price, Fun Palace project, illustration from *New Scientist*, May 1964; 41b Cedric Price, Fun Palace project, illustration from *Architectural Review*, January 1965; 45t Digital Image © The Museum of Modern Art/Licensed by SCALA / Art Resource, NY; 45cl Shadrach Woods, diagram for Berlin Free University project, 1964. *Perspecta* 11 (1967); 45cr Konrad Waschmann, Experimental Structural Web, 1953. *Arts and Architecture*, May 1967; 45b Konrad Waschsmann, interlocking organization of design studio teams, 1959. Wachsmann, *Wendepunkt im Bauen*, Krausskopt-Verlag, Wiesbaden, 1959, 206; 48 Konrad Waschsmann, Building Research Division organization, 1965. *Arts and Architecture*, May 1967; 49t Konrad Waschsmann, "Spatial expansion of categories of facts, subject matters and relations," 1965. *Arts and Architecture*, May 1967; 49c Konrad Waschsmann, University Organization, 1965. *Arts and Architecture*, May 1967; 49b "What happens when information rubs against information...," Marshall Mcluhan, *The Medium is the Massage*, 1967; 9, 51tl Illustration from John Entenza, "What is a House?" *Arts and Architecture*, July 1944; 51tr *Österreichische Friedrich und Lillian Kiesler Privatstiftung*, Vienna; 10, 51b Friedrich Kiesler, Morphology-Chart, *Architectural Record*, September 1939.

Redefining Network Paradigms

55t, 55b, 57t, 60–61, 75 Courtesy Anthony Burke; 57b, 72–73 Beau Trincia, "Ambient Structure" thesis, UC Berkeley, architecture 2006; 12–13, 64–65, 67 Courtesy of Pierogi and Donald Lombardi. Whitney Museum of American Art, New York. Purchased with funds from the Drawing Committee and the Contemporary Committee; 11, 69lt, 69lc Installation by Anthony Burke and Eric Paulos, with the help of Tom Jenkins and Karen Marcelo at SFMoMA, October 2005. Photograph by Anthony Burke; 69rt, 69rb Courtesy Jake Applebaum; 69lc Photograph by Alex Roberts

Biological Networks: On Neurons, Cellular Automata, and Relational Architectures

79, 83, 87 From Stephen Wolfram, *A New Kind of Science* (Champaign, IL: Wolfram Media, 2002). © Wolfram Research, Inc (The use of Wolfram Research, Inc. images does not imply in anyway their endorsement of their work.); 14, 91 Courtesy of IBM/EPFL Blue Brain Project; 95t From Benjamin

Aranda and Chris Lasch, *Pamphlet Architecture 27: Tooling* (New York: Princeton Architectural Press, 2006), 38. © 2006 Princeton Architectural Press; 15, 95b Courtesy of Achim Menges; 97 Courtesy of Jun Yu

Scalar Networks, Super Creeps: Approaching the Non-Standard in the Architecture of Servo

All images courtesy servo

Stop Motion Studies

All images courtesy the author

Material Agency

121t, 129 © Testa & Weiser, 2006; 121b, 124–125 © Emergent Design Group/Testa, 2000; 127t © Emergent Design Group, 1998; 18, 127b © Emergent Design Group, 2001

The Dom-in[f]o House

All images courtesy the author

From Data to Its Organizing Structure

All images courtesy the author

Beyond Code

23, 167lt, 167lc, 170–171, 173, 175tl, 175c, 175b Courtesy the author; 167lb, 167rt, 167rb Courtesy of bitforms gallery, New York; 175tr Courtesy of BANK Gallery, Los Angeles

Climbing through Complexity Ceilings

187tl, 188t © 1997 Peter Bentley; 187tr, 191bl, 191br © 2003, 2004 Ramona Behravan 187b, 188br © 2003, 2004 Siavash Haroun Mahdavi; 188bl Image produced by the racing simulator *Electronic Arts™ Formula One Challenge '99–'00*. Work by Krzysztof Wloch, 2004; 191t © 2002 Sanjeev Kumar; 192–193 © 2004 David Malkin

Multi-National City: Inside Outsourcing

199t, 206, 207t, 209 Courtesy Martin/Baxi Architects; 199c (199c), 199b, 203 Courtesy the author; 24, 207b Courtesy Urtzi Grau

Contributor Biographies

Peter J. Bentley is a senior research fellow and college teacher at the Department of Computer Science, University College London (UCL), where he runs the Digital Biology Interest Group. His research investigates evolutionary algorithms, ecological modelling, artificial immune systems, computational development and swarming systems, applied to diverse applications including design, control, novel robotics, fraud detection, security, and music composition. He is editor of the books *Evolutionary Design by Computers*, *Creative Evolutionary Systems*, and *On Growth, Form and Computers*, and is author of the popular science book *Digital Biology*.

Anthony Burke is a designer and assistant professor in architecture at the University of California, Berkeley, specializing in digital and new media design theory and techniques and their implications for architecture and urbanism. He has worked as an architect and educator in Hong Kong, New York, San Francisco, and Sydney, and is currently collaborating with the Intel Research Lab at Berkeley on projects in urban computing. He is the principal of Offshorestudio.net, a research and design practice dedicated to exploring the relationship between network culture, urban computing, and architecture.

David Crawford studied film, video, and new media at the Massachusetts College of Art and received a BFA in 1997. In 1999, his *Here and Now* project was commissioned by New Radio and Performing Arts with funds from National Endowment for the Arts. In 2000, his *Light of Speed* project was a finalist for the SFMoMA Webby Prize for Excellence in Online Art. In 2003, his *Stop Motion Studies* project received an Artport Gate Page Commission from the Whitney Museum of American Art and an Award of Distinction in the Net Vision category at the Prix Ars Electronica.

Christopher Hight is an assistant professor at the Rice School of Architecture, where he is pursuing design research on human and non-human co-mingling located at the nexus between ecologies of development, networked organizations, and landscape. He has been a Fulbright Scholar and obtained a Masters degree in the histories and theories of architecture from the Architectural Association, and a PhD from the London Consortium at the University of London. He is currently finishing a book on cybernetics, formalism, and postwar architectural design, and is co-editor of *AD: Collective Intelligence in Design*.

George Legrady is professor of interactive media, with joint appointment in the Media Arts & Technology program and the Department of Art, UC Santa Barbara. He has previously held full-time appointments at the Merz Akademie, Institute for Visual Communication, Stuttgart, the Conceptual Design/Information Arts program, San Francisco State University, University of Southern California, and the University of Western Ontario. His creative work as won numerous awards and grants from the Creative Capital Foundation; the Daniel Langlois Foundation for the Arts, Science and Technology, Montreal; the Canada Council; and the NEA, among many others.

Reinhold Martin is associate professor of architecture at Columbia University, where he directs the PhD program in architecture and the Master of Science program in advanced architectural design. He is also a partner in the firm Martin/Baxi Architects and a founding co-editor of the journal *Grey Room*. He is the author of *The Organizational Complex: Architecture, Media, and Corporate Space* and the co-author, with Kadambari Baxi, of *Entropia* and *Multi-National City: Architectural Itineraries*.

C. E. B. Reas is an artist and educator exploring abstract kinetic systems through diverse digital media. He received his Master of Science degree in Media Arts and Sciences from MIT, where he was a member of the Aesthetics and Computation Group. Reas is currently an Assistant Professor in UCLA's Design | Media Arts department.

Dagmar Richter is a professor of architecture and urban studies at UCLA, and has a long teaching pedigree, including schools such as the Rhode Island School of Design, the Cooper Union, the Harvard School of Design, Columbia University, and the Academy of Art in Berlin. Her design firm is based in both Los Angeles and Berlin, has won prizes in international design competitions, and has been exhibited extensively in the United States and Europe. In 2001 Princeton Architectural Press published a monograph on her work, *XYZ: The Architecture of Dagmar Richter*.

Michael Speaks has published and lectured internationally on art, architecture, urban design, and scenario planning. He is the founding editor of *Polygraph* and has been the senior editor at *ANY* magazine and the series editor for *Writing Architecture*. He is also a contributing editor for *Architectural Record* and serves on the editorial advisory board of *a+u* and on the advisory board for the Storefront for Art and Architecture in New York. He is currently head of the Metropolitan Research and Design Post Graduate Degree at the Southern California Institute of Architecture in Los Angeles, and heads the Los Angeles–based urban research group BIG SOFT ORANGE.

Peter Testa is design principal at Testa & Weiser in Los Angeles, where he leads a wide range of projects including Carbon Tower with ARUP; and CYAN, a biodegradable building system using nano-cellulose and engineered composite wood structures with EMPA Switzerland. He has held academic and research positions at Columbia University, Harvard University GSD, and the Massachusetts Institute of Technology. He is the recipient of numerous awards including the Design Arts Award of the National Endowment for the Arts and the MIT Innovation in Teaching Award. The *London Times* and BBC recently profiled his firm at the forefront of companies shaping the future of architecture.

Therese Tierney is currently a doctoral candidate at University of California Berkeley. During 2005, she studied at Massachusetts Institute of Technology Media Laboratory, where she was engaged in design research on computational systems. An award-winning architect and design instructor, Tierney is also the author of *Abstract Space: Beneath the Media Surface* (forthcoming in 2007).

Devyn Weiser is a founding partner and design principal of the Los Angeles–based firm Testa & Weiser. Her work ranges from fashion and product design to large-scale architecture. Recent buildings and projects include an all-composite structure for an apparel shop in West Hollywood; "Sound Lounge" for Totem Design in SoHo; and a pair of contour taped carbon fiber beach houses in Southern California. Exhibitions of her work include shows at the New Museum of Contemporary Art in New York; Cooper-Hewitt National Design Museum; and the Los Angeles Museum of Contemporary Art. She is currently a member of the design faculty at SCI-Arc.

Mark Wigley is dean of the Graduate School of Architecture, Preservation and Planning at Columbia University. He is the author of *The Architecture of Deconstruction: Derrida's Haunt*; *White Walls, Designer Dresses: The Fashioning of Modern Architecture*; and *Constant's New Babylon: The Hyper-Architecture of Desire*. He is also co-editor of *The Activist Drawing: Retracing Situationist Architectures from Constant's New Babylon to Beyond*, and is currently preparing a pre-history of virtual space.